W9-CUC-888

YOUR
Home
YOUR
Style

YOUR
Home
YOUR
Style

HOW TO FIND YOUR LOOK
& CREATE ROOMS YOU LOVE

DONNA GARLOUGH

Photography by Joyelle West

RIZZOLI
NEW YORK

New York Paris London Milan

FOR

SARAH & JONAH

MAY YOU STYLE
YOUR OWN LIVES WITH LOVE,
LIGHT, AND PURPOSE

&

FOR

DAVID

A DREAM WEAVER LIKE
NONE OTHER

CONTENTS

INTRODUCTION

The urge to decorate has always been in my blood, or perhaps more accurately, in my garage. My mother, who immigrated to the United States from Vietnam, spent the 1980s importing and selling home accents from Asia and storing the excess inventory at home, where other people park their cars. I remember wriggling between shelves stacked high with bookends and vases and porcelain urns after school; trips to trade shows, where she sold her wares to retailers; and weekend mornings at auctions in Los Angeles, where she fought off other bidders for the perfect cane-back settee for our own living room. Nesting made her happy, as did helping others nest.

My mother never had any design training—she simply loved decorating. Somehow I inherited that gene, as I always wanted to personalize my own space. I went from draping my college dorm room in $5 batik sarongs to making my own beaded pendant lamps inspired by ones I saw at a favorite restaurant to eventually buying and renovating one home before starting over with another. I worked for magazines, interviewed other people about their homes, and wrote their stories; I started putting products together for trend stories and photo shoots at the office and created my own decor narratives at home, too.

Today, I help lots of people decorate their homes on a daily basis. And I mean *daily*—I'm the style director for Joss & Main, an online home-decor retailer that presents new looks on our website every single day.

I never feel like I'm selling something, though. Instead, I'm putting together great stuff in new and interesting ways for people to admire and maybe, hopefully, say, "Yes! Aha! That's me! I want that!"

But there's a gap between wanting and doing, and that gap is what prompted me to write this book. In this age of flash sales, Pinterest, and incredibly gorgeous home-design blogs and magazines, there's no shortage of inspiration, and we clip and save our ideas like madmen, don't we? Yet what we need is more than pretty pictures squirreled away in a folder, virtual or tangible. What we need is the guts to decorate our own homes.

For reasons I've never understood, people don't feel qualified to decorate without feeling like hacks. They apologize for themselves before they've even picked up a curtain rod, saying things like "I don't know what I'm doing. I don't know if this is going to go together. I'm not a decorator."

Here's why this is illogical: No one says "but I'm not a chef" before he or she makes dinner. You may not have years of culinary training or an apprenticeship in sauces, but that shouldn't stop you from making a damn good plate of pasta for your friends. Anyone can cook, and anyone can decorate. Reading tips online and in books will help you get better, and so will magazines and design shows. But nothing will teach you how to do something like getting up and doing it, occasionally stopping to critique your own work. Trust me, the more you practice, the better you'll get.

Thanks to a variety of luxe textures—herringbone mosaic backsplash tiles, marbleized porcelain countertops, glistening crystal, and the rough edges of an oversize shell—a monochrome white kitchen is anything but plain.

It's no surprise we have so many seeds of doubt. Misconceptions abound in the design world (for example, that you should always "invest" in permanent pieces like beds and sofas, and you shouldn't spend money on good furniture for a rental). Sure, those tenets held true for previous generations, when store options were limited, most furniture was handmade, and people bought forever homes as newlyweds. Over the last decade, though, both the marketplace and our lifestyle have vastly changed, making shopping an ever more diverse and dynamic experience. There's no right way to shop anymore.

So instead of listening to—or worse, repeating—these outdated dictates and refrains of self-doubt, why not adopt a new set of decorating truths that will give you the confidence and permission you need to start creating a space you love? Here are the design rules I think everyone should adopt.

A WELL-STYLED HOME will look great even in its natural state.

1 IT'S ALWAYS A GOOD TIME TO DECORATE.

Whether you're renting or renovating, staying or going, it's time. Just because your surroundings may change doesn't mean you shouldn't love where you are right now, or that you have to suffer a space you despise. Your future plans should be a guardrail that helps direct the style and cost of your current purchases, not a roadblock to any kind of decorating at all.

2 EVERYONE NEEDS A ROOM MOCK-UP.

A room mock-up is a place to store your leading ideas and visualize how your space and items work together. Whether it's digital or analog (such as a bulletin board or a wall you tape pictures to), the mock-up is an integral part of any do-it-yourself design project. While online pinboards and bookmarks can be helpful, there's nothing like seeing your design choices all in one place. It's a living document that you'll use, change, and change again as your vague ideas morph into real-life rooms in 3-D.

3 THE BEST STYLE IS REAL-WORLD STYLE.

As someone who's been on set and crafted some of those perfectly balanced, ideally accessorized images you're bookmarking, I'm here to tell you why you can stop comparing your home to the ones in catalogs and magazines. Part of creating your dream home is realizing you're going to be awake in it—eating in it, cooking in it, cleaning in it—and making adjustments to make it work for real life. Outside of photo-shoot hours, nobody has a pantry stocked only with grains in shades of beige. Nobody sane coordinates the fruit in their fruit bowl with the utensil crock on the counter. Nobody—except me, and I'm not always sane—buys only neutral-colored shampoo bottles. There's no need to compare your everyday home to a professionally primped one; a well-styled home will look great even in its natural state.

Placing fresh flowers around the house is one of the easiest ways to elevate a home's look and feel. You don't even have to be a pro at arrangements: Single-variety, single-color bunches always look clean and classic.

4 NOTHING IS PERMANENT.

One of the biggest hurdles for paralyzed decorators is the concept of permanence: *If I spend X dollars on a sofa, then I have to get X years out of it so that it's "worth" it.* That's a logic handed down from past generations, and it just doesn't hold true anymore. Most of the furniture built for the mass market today pales in comparison quality-wise to what our grandparents bought and won't last as long as we want it to. It's also easier than ever to sell something you don't want: If you take care of your stuff, you can usually sell it online or locally for half of what you paid, or give it to charity and take the tax write-off. Or you can turn furniture upcycling into dinner theater, like I do. I live in a city full of resourceful picker-uppers and college students scrounging for free stuff. I love to put things on the curb, pour myself a glass of wine, and sit by the window, watching people take things away. It's cathartic, really. The bottom line is, you get to choose how long you cohabitate with the things you buy. You're not beholden to your stuff. Set it free.

5 CHALLENGES BREED CREATIVITY.

Whether it's an oddly shaped room that defies common seating plans, pets preventing you from purchasing the velvet sofa you admire, or a shoestring budget, a design limitation can be a blessing. Challenges force you to do something very good, which is slow the heck down and think about what you really need and want now in this space. Instead of storming into a furniture store and buying the first living room set you like, you have to stop and think, *Is this right for my daily routine? Will this fit in my doors? How will this look with the stuff in the adjacent room?* It can force you to do some research beforehand, and that gives you time to test out different looks in your room mock-up. It can also lead you to consider less conventional furniture combinations, such as a modern sofa with a vintage chair, because that's what fits your life, budget, and space. Ultimately, challenges mean you'll spend more time on the process of design, which translates to a greater chance of loving the home you end up with.

◀◀ A vintage rattan peacock chair, originally purchased for the homeowners' wedding, now reigns in the corner of a guest room. Accents with a handmade feel— Japanese shibori (tie-dyed) prints, an indigo pillow, and a distressed Oriental rug—lend color and charm.

How to Use This Book

This book is not about showing you looks you might like or telling you which pillow to put with which sofa. Those are fun topics, but being spoon-fed design rules won't help you get more comfortable designing your own space or shopping for decor. My hope is that this book will force a bit of self-reflection and make you stop and ask, What do I want out of my home, and how do I get there? And by stopping to reflect, you'll gradually unshackle yourself from any preconceived notions that are keeping you from creating your dream home.

Need proof that you can decorate without formal training? All of the spaces photographed for these pages belong to non-designers. They're simply homes created by people who took the time to think about their own needs, who gradually cultivated an aesthetic, and who trusted their guts along the way. You'll see the eclectic living room of Kelly, a family-and-wedding photographer living in a sleepy seaside community; the sub-urban Colonial home of Alisa, a fashion consultant; and the funky little farmhouse owned by Emily, an event planner. One colorful city row house belongs to Cristy, an artist and entrepreneur, and her husband, Alex, a musician. Jamie, a psychiatrist, and her husband Jon-Luc, an attorney, masterminded the renovation of their own urban townhome. And me? Well, I'm a magazine editor who stumbled into the decor business and never, ever looked back.

As you read the first five chapters of this book, you'll gain an under-standing of how your design mind is wired—your design disposition—and you'll learn to put some words behind your style. From there, you'll learn how to utilize a room mock-up, and you'll get some specifics to help you create the experiences, aesthetics, and feelings you want at home. That legwork will allow you to shop and arrange on a timeline that works for your life and bud-get. You'll learn what kind of decorator you are, find your design strengths, and know when to let your gut be your guide. My hope, at the end of this jour-ney, is that you will not just end up with a really pretty space—you'll also view your home, and your role in creating it, with joy and confidence.

▶▶ Despite its very upright architecture, this New England home feels breezy and relaxed thanks to the owners' bright and eclectic decor. A utilitarian cart offers storage and serves as a joint console and plant stand in the hallway; a peek into the dining room reveals a host of decidedly nontraditional furnishings.

From built-in bookshelves to mantels, walls, and sofas, every corner is a style opportunity. Here, the ocean-loving homeowners infused a blank-slate living room with a cozy coastal vibe via wall art, surf- and sea-themed books, and decor in shades of sandy pink and navy blue.

And what does that confidence look like, exactly? To me, a good indicator is whether or not a person will go out and buy a matching bedroom set—the twin nightstands, coordinating bed frame, and nearly identical dresser you see in every 1950s movie. Manufacturers and stores love selling them, because they make three times the sale, and customers keep buying them because they think that's what grown-ups are supposed to do, and they're scared to do anything else. Confident buyers, however, will break up the set and decide which parts of it work for them. It's not about being cocky or assured of one's rightness. It's about being confident. Even professional interior designers can never know for sure; that's why they bring five rugs to a client's house and try them all out in the room. Rather, confidence is the ability to act on instincts—to show a willingness to be different and to turn down the upsell. To ignore what grown-ups do. To say, "I'd like to try this my way."

I love, love, love to help people discover their own way. Let's go find yours.

PART

ONE

FINDING

YOUR

STYLE

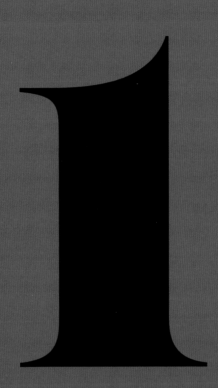

WHAT'S YOUR DESIGN DISPOSITION?

THE FIVE DESIGN PERSONALITIES

PREVIOUS SPREAD: Grouping smaller decorative items, like candlesticks and trinket boxes, on a tray gives them presence and makes their placement feel intentional. **OPPOSITE:** Flanking a fireplace with two facing chairs transforms an open space into a more intimate conversation area. The chairs, bought on sale from a big-box store, were previously a tame gray but are now exuberant in fuchsia velvet.

In my early twenties, while working as an editor at Martha Stewart's green-minded magazine *Whole Living*, I garnered a cursory introduction to the Eastern approach to wellness known as Ayurveda. The ancient Indian healing system classifies everyone into one of three doshas, or mind-body types: Maybe you're a sprightly and energetic vata; a gentle but sluggish kapha; or a headstrong and passionate pitta. You can possess qualities of two doshas, the thinking goes, but most everyone has a dominant type, and knowing it is the key to bringing your mind, body, and environment into balance.

After years of interviewing homeowners about their spaces, talking to interior designers about themselves and their clients, and seeing friends and colleagues work through their own decorating dilemmas, I've concluded that the idea of having inherent dispositions applies to how we design our homes as well. To be able to design your home effectively, you need to step back and try to understand your innate leanings and how they lead to the design challenges you face. Without a little self-reflection, you're likely to carry your unique combination of concerns, aspirations, and hang-ups from home to home, and project to project, until you get tired of spending money, give up on decorating, or call in a professional.

I've observed that people have one of five distinct design dispositions: There are Self-Expressionists, Pragmatists, Historians, Dream Weavers, and Tinkerers. Your disposition defines what kind of design creature you are, and it affects everything about how you nest. Do you crave welcoming warmth or cooling calm? Do you like to attack projects slowly and methodically, carefully considering each decision on the way, or do you arrive at your best ideas via an impulsive, creative whirlwind? A quiz at the end of this chapter will help you identify your type.

My disposition? I like to tinker . When I was a tween, it wasn't uncommon for me to lock myself in my room in a fit of pubescent rage and start moving things around. Bewildered, my mother would open the door and discover I'd completely changed the floor plan. For me, decorating is therapeutic—if I can't reorganize my emotions, I can at least reorganize my environment. And so I live in a constantly changing home that thrills and frustrates me every day as I move from one decor project to the next. I grow bored, I redecorate, and I don't think I'll ever stop—and that's OK. I've arrived at a decorating strategy that allows me to cycle objects through my home, from one room to the next and from desktop to mantel. Instead of simply acquiring things en masse, I rearrange and slowly incorporate new finds into my arsenal. I've given up on trying to find my forever-favorite pieces and their permanent locations within my home. They don't exist.

This frustrated my husband for years. To him, decor is something that complements a home's architecture and increases its value, that communicates quality, and that gets done once and done right. And so rather than investing in the chesterfield he's always admired—or trying to find one at a more palatable price—his tendency is to put off decorating indefinitely and live with a hodgepodge of purely functional furniture, maintaining that he'll decorate "properly" and strategically at a later date. That I'd spend money on a piece I loved but didn't quite know what to do with seemed nonsensical. However, after a decade of seeing me stage a whole house for an appraisal or sale using random decor I've pulled out of closets and moved from room to room, he's come around. And I've come up with a system that lets him get a peek at the end state of my design plans for each room as I plan it out.

My friend Kim is like neither my husband nor me. She will search long and hard for each individual piece she brings home, heirloom or casual. She decides exactly what she wants, then watches sales like a hawk so she can swoop in and buy exactly that piece at the price she wants to pay. She won't buy another sofa or reorganize her space until she has to, either because she's moving or because the things she has are nearly threadbare. While she enjoys decorating, it's more of a necessity than a hobby for her, so she does it and moves on.

Your DISPOSITION defines what kind of design CREATURE you are and affects everything about how you NEST.

◀◀ Do you gravitate toward quirky decor that begs guests to ask, "Where'd you get that?" (Case in point: a flocked green cockatoo.) If you do, chances are, you're part Self-Expressionist.

THE FIVE
DESIGN
DISPOSITIONS

1
THE SELF-EXPRESSIONIST

*You want your home
to be a reflection of your
personality.*

YOUR STRENGTHS
collecting one-of-a-kind
items, making "I have to have that"
buys that you don't necessarily
know how you'll use

YOUR BIGGEST CHALLENGES
pulling it all together into
one core look that reflects who you
are right now, feeling
confident about your purchases

2
THE PRAGMATIST

*You want to decorate
each space once and never think
about it again.*

YOUR STRENGTHS
setting and sticking to
a budget, executing a plan quickly
and methodically

YOUR BIGGEST CHALLENGES
blocking off time to
craft your plan, making spot
decisions when every choice
feels permanent

3
THE HISTORIAN

*You want every piece
in your home to tell a story.*

YOUR STRENGTHS
finding quality items,
being true to a design era or
historical home

YOUR BIGGEST CHALLENGES
feeling like everything
has to be heirloom
(or heirloom-quality), getting rid
of items that have a past

4
THE DREAM WEAVER

*You want a transporting look that
reflects your surroundings and
makes coming home feel like going
on a chic retreat.*

YOUR STRENGTHS
knowing the exact vibe
you're going for, pulling wholesale
looks you love from a catalog

YOUR BIGGEST CHALLENGES
combining your dream-home
buys with items you already own,
taking your time

5
THE TINKERER

You want everything you see.

YOUR STRENGTHS
buying items simply
because you love them, arranging
and rearranging as the
mood strikes

YOUR BIGGEST CHALLENGES
not succumbing to
trends, thinking your buying
decisions through, never
feeling "done"

Kim's a Pragmatist. My husband is a Historian. And I'm a Tinkerer, with a bit of Self-Expressionist thrown in. Knowing which of these design dispositions best describes you is the first step in a successful design journey and will help save you—and your home—from your own worst tendencies. The guide at left will help you recognize your type.

It's possible that you find yourself not fitting squarely into any one of these types. Like me, you might be a blend of two. The following quiz will help you determine which design disposition(s) you are.

⬆ Displaying a collection of like items in a wee vignette is a perfect way for Historians, Self-Expressionists, and Tinkerers to play with their decor. Think of the pieces as cast members on a stage, grouping them in pairs and clusters with tall items in back and small ones out front.

DISCOVER

YOUR

DESIGN

DISPOSITION

Circle the choice that describes you most closely.

My ideal home shopping trip is...

A An afternoon spent wandering in a foreign city, picking up things that will remind me of this trip long after.

B A walk through a neatly organized store where things are easy to find, and where I can get everything I need in a single visit.

C A treasure hunt in an antiques shop or estate sale.

D A trip to a shop that immediately feels like "me" and is perfect for my lifestyle.

E Discovering a new decor store that's full of things I've never seen before.

When reading magazines or surfing online, I find myself bookmarking a lot of...

A Gallery walls and styled bookshelves.

B Pantries, entries, and laundry rooms.

C Historic renovations.

D Master suites and vacation homes.

E "Hacks" or unconventional ways to use items you already have.

I'm most inspired by...

A My own experiences.

B How-to articles.

C Stories of how designs came to be.

D Hotels and luxury spaces.

E Color and trend stories.

I'd be unhappiest in...

A A fully furnished home I couldn't change.

B A house with a bad floor plan.

C A large, modern building or neighborhood of identical dwellings.

D A house with no curb appeal.

E An outdated rental that I couldn't change.

I'd love to live in...

A A home full of photos and memories.

B A well-built, well-maintained house in a neighborhood I love.

C That house from my favorite classic movie.

D A sprawling home in my favorite vacation spot.

E Several different cities, with a different look in every one of my homes.

The books you're likely to find on my coffee table...

A Explore my travels, studies, and hobbies.

B Are the ones people actually pick up and read.

C Are a deep dive into obscure topics.

D Have great covers and titles.

E Change by the week.

The best restaurant interiors...

A Remind me of a favorite trip, meal, or memory.

B Are ultra-comfortable, with great seats, lighting, and the right size crowd.

C Have lots of great details and possibly a backstory to the building.

D Make me feel like I'm somewhere else entirely.

E Are new and buzzing with stylish people.

My perfect bed would...

A Have layers of pattern and texture.

B Keep me cozy and be easy to make in the morning.

C Be a refurbished antique, heirloom piece, or expertly crafted reproduction.

D Feel like a hotel bed.

E Have mix-and-match layers I can tailor to the season.

The first thing I read in a magazine is...

A The story that relates to my life.

B The table of contents.

C The long feature.

D Nothing. I look at the pictures first.

E Never the same—I flip around.

On social media, I'm most likely to "like" or "favorite" a...

A Quote.

B Brilliant storage idea.

C Makeover.

D Photo of a luxury home or resort.

E "10 Ways to Wear..." fashion graphic.

Now, take a look at your answers and see which letters you chose most often.

Mostly As:
SELF-EXPRESSIONIST

Mostly Bs:
PRAGMATIST

Mostly Cs:
HISTORIAN

Mostly Ds:
DREAM WEAVER

Mostly Es:
TINKERER

Know now which disposition(s) suits you best? Great. Go back and take another look at each disposition's strengths and challenges, listed on page 30. Then keep these tendencies in mind as you start to build your plan in the next few chapters and, more importantly, as you shop. The rest will unfold as you go. The key is to remember that not everyone designs by the same rules, even if we all have the same goal of creating a home that we love.

CHAPTER

DEFINING YOUR AESTHETIC

FIGURING OUT WHAT YOU LIKE

PREVIOUS SPREAD: A tray of decor on an ottoman can be whisked away for a more easygoing, put-your-feet-up vibe. OPPOSITE: Teal velvet chairs bring a dose of tempered glamour to a renovated Tudor home. A tall bird of paradise plant fills out a bare corner, breaks up a sea of white walls, and helps balance out the deep color in the lower half of the room.

One evening after a local fund-raiser in my neighborhood, I was approached by a fellow city dweller who was at a crossroads in putting together her new home with her fiancé. "I know what I like," she told me, "but it's just so hard to describe, and it's even harder to put together." As I prodded her about what vibe she wanted in her home, she grappled, tossing out the names of certain designers, certain terms she knew from magazines, and certain stores, qualifying each by saying it wasn't 100 percent "her." Instead, she felt attached to each of the looks in different ways, and she ultimately wanted her home to be mix of all of them.

Isn't this how many of us start out—and what we continue to struggle with as we shop, nest, and renovate? Making up one's own mix seems *so* hard—something only professionals are qualified to do. We hope and pray that there's some sort of prefab combination out there that we just haven't found yet. We search for our design analogues—the magazine, blogger, or TV-makeover guru whose style suits us perfectly. We take diagnostic quizzes online to see if our style is "midcentury modern with a Scandinavian twist," "formal English traditional," or "bohemian glamour," as though knowing that string of terms will help you feel more confident as you navigate a store or website.

Bull, I say. Unless you have a deep understanding of those abstract design terms, I don't believe they give most people an enhanced strategy for furnishing their homes. Here's why:

None of the blanket design terms ever seem to fit anyone exactly. Sure, maybe you love the midcentury look of the *Mad Men* sets and think that's what you want in your space, but what do you do if you stumble upon the occasional piece that's *not* that style and love it? Should you doubt whether it belongs in your space? Should you pass on it because it's not what the expert of your style would have chosen? Just as everyone's wardrobe includes items for work, weekends, and vacations, one's home style is hardly ever one-note.

Style terminology sans visuals can be extremely misleading. People have vastly different interpretations of design terms—or inaccurate perceptions of what they mean. While chatting with a business partner who was moving into a new home, she told me she wanted her house to be "contemporary, relaxing, and Zen." I imagined a minimalist, Eastern-inspired home—someplace sleek and almost Japanese-inspired. But when she showed me pictures of items she liked and had bought for her space, what I saw was industrial-style furniture, accents with urban glamour, and cushy, cozy textiles. Same terms, different interpretations.

Design terminology doesn't help you in the store. Whether you go online or to a brick-and-mortar retailer, shopping for the home is designed to be an immersive experience. There's a ton to look at, and things are put together in ways that make you want everything you see. If you've defined your style too specifically, you might pick up a throw pillow and ask, "Is this bohemian modern? Because I'm bohemian modern." You might then see another pillow and not know if it's any more right. Even terms like *traditional* and *glamorous* can be unhelpful, especially if you're trying to pick something other than furniture, such as bath towels or a solid-colored duvet.

Hyper-defined style can feel forced. The best homes speak to the owner's personality, not just an aesthetic point of view. Even if a magazine article or quiz tells you that "feminine cottage" or "Moroccan exotic" is your look, holding too closely to a theme can make your home seem like, well, a theme park, especially if the schema has been hatched by someone else. The worst part? The more narrow a style you carve out for yourself, the more likely you'll change your mind about it later.

◄◄ You don't need much space to showcase your style. Here, a simple combination of a treasured photo, pretty foliage, a keepsake box, and a lamp embodies this homeowner's affinity for rich neutrals and meaningful decor.

➤ Pinterest and Instagram may keep design inspiration at your fingertips, but there's no replacing the power of print. Look beyond home-decor magazines alone, and don't be afraid to take cues from catalogs, travel mags, fashion issues, and more.

DESIGN
REVELATION
№ **1**

Props Change Everything

It happens all the time. Friends say, "I want a colorful home!" or "I love how bright, bold, and cheerful this room is!" But the colorful homes they love in magazines and on TV are often more muted in real life than they are in print or on your screen. As you review pictures, take note of what, exactly, is bringing color to the space: Is it a bunch of red dahlias on the white kitchen counter, a matching red colander on the open shelves, and red tea towels draped over the counter stools? Those are nonpermanent touches, probably put there by a stylist right before the shoot. Try to distinguish between what "lives" in the space (like furniture, curtain fabrics, and paint) and what's just there for the pictures. If it turns out you like your color in nonpermanent splashes, consider taking that same approach to styling your own home—and think twice before painting that cherry-red accent wall or buying a ruby-hued sofa.

So how *do* you define your look? How do you identify the pieces you'll love in your home as well as in the store?

Easy—pretend you're your own design client. When most interior designers take on a new project, there's usually a bit of homework required by the customer. The homeowner is asked to save and share images from magazines or the Internet, which the designer then interprets when designing the complete new space, before layering in his or her expert advice and ideas. But who's to say you can't approximate the homework-and-analysis process by yourself and cultivate a little design awareness of your own?

Start by identifying twenty to thirty images of spaces you love. And I mean *love*: not over-the-top mansions or resorts you'd like to visit someday, but rooms you can see being part of your own home and lifestyle. Don't worry about whether they go together or how much they cost, just browse and save. For example, when I was working on my house, I flagged bedrooms with loads of built-in storage, sitting rooms with funky antique chandeliers, sofas and love seats that I wanted to curl up in, and kitchens where I could see myself cooking a meal and pouring wine for friends. I even saved photographs of hotel rooms, libraries, and lobbies.

Once you have a good collection of rooms you love, it's time to decode your picks: As you look at each image, consider what it tells you about where you stand on each of the following factors.

FACTOR № 1
YOUR COLOR TOLERANCE

Chances are, most of your saved shots will fall into one or two of these categories. (If they don't, set them aside in another folder or location where you can reference them later. They might help inform the nuances of your decorating approach after you've determined your broader strategy.)

- **LEVEL 1: A Blank Slate.** Most of the rooms you like are nearly color-free, built around one pale shade like white or cream, or one dark shade, like charcoal gray.

- **LEVEL 2: Neutral Territory.** If these rooms were a closet, they'd be a mixed but muted assortment of white, black, gray, and beige, perhaps with a little navy or camel built in.

- **LEVEL 3: Careful Contrast.** Whether it's a pair of bold lamps, a set of pillows, or a dramatic canvas on the wall, your favorite rooms are mostly neutral but punctuated by a strong accent color.

- **LEVEL 4: Lovely Layers.** You're not color-shy, but you don't like a lot of variety, either. If there's blue on the walls, there's also blue on the pillows, rug, and wall art. You might even do some upholstered seating in a non-neutral shade, but you like to keep colors in the same family.

- **LEVEL 5: Lots of Pop.** These rooms have a bit of indigo here and some spicy orange there. You like the vibrancy that several strong hues can bring to a space.

- **LEVEL 6: A Bevy of Brights.** You're fearless when it comes to color, and your favorite rooms are splashed with a near-rainbow of shades.

FACTOR № 2
YOUR FAVORITE FINISHES AND MATERIALS

Do all of the rooms you love contain marble? Is gnarly driftwood in all your spaces, or is everything painted white? We often gravitate toward the same features repeatedly. So look closely: Maybe you're a sucker for kitchens with brass hardware or vintage-inspired details like Edison bulbs. Maybe all of your rooms contain antiques. Make a list of these features, and let it be your conscience when you get distracted by pretty things in stores or online.

◀◀ The most interesting interiors incorporate their owners' passions in understated ways. Here, outdoor chairs adorned with rope knots lend a coastal home a subtle nautical vibe.

FACTOR № 3
YOUR FORMALITY LEVEL

Do you want your home to feel like a wave, a handshake, or a hug? This is not a trick question: Some people adore spaces that feel worthy of high-end magazine pages and dinner parties (aka the wave), while others want spaces that beckon you to take off your shoes and flop down on the sofa, drink in hand (aka the hug). Some people want something in between. Once you zero in on a formality level, you'll be better equipped to make decisions on things like seating and decor.

FACTOR № 4
YOUR DESIRE FOR DRAMA

If you tend to choose rooms with standout architectural features, moody lighting, and statement decor pieces (think a bold pillow that jumps off the sofa, a breathtaking rug, or a chandelier that owns the room), you've got an appetite for drama. However, if you like rooms that feel more balanced and soothing, you crave harmony. Knowing this will help you decide how much pattern and color to bring into your space and how you can play with scale (say, a huge light fixture or a big mirror in an interesting shape) to create more or less visual impact.

FACTOR № 5
WHETHER YOU'RE A MIXER OR A MATCHER

Are you drawn to rooms that feel as if they were consciously put together around a pattern or color scheme? Do rooms feel more "right" to you when the art coordinates with the painted wall behind it and when the pillows and window coverings coordinate? You're a matcher. If you'd rather look at a room and say "That's such a surprising, unique, or quirky pairing," you're made to mix. Knowing this will help you jump more easily from one decor decision to the next and build your room in layers that align with your ultimate home goals.

▸ A tiny powder room becomes a major statement space when clad in a bold marble-effect wallpaper. While a big print isn't for the faint of heart, sticking to a "safe" palette (blue and white) and just two metal finishes (weathered brass and shiny chrome) makes it easier to pull off a funky yet pulled-together look.

If your tastes lean modern but you've accumulated items with a more traditional feel, displaying them in spare arrangements—white bookshelves, lots of negative space—and mixing in pieces with cleaner silhouettes can give them a more contemporary feel.

Where you stand on the above factors comprises your design style. Regarding color, I'd consider myself a level three because I gravitate toward neutrals but *looooove* a rich color statement, like a navy wall. My favorite materials are velvet, linen, marble, and brass, as well as textiles with a handmade texture, like worn antique rugs or hand-dyed pillows. My formality level is a handshake—I like a pretty formal look, but I don't want things to feel untouchable. Drama? Bring it on. And I'm definitely a mixer; I admire the coordinated-pillows-and-curtains thing from afar, but my home is more of a layering game.

Admittedly, this is a lot to keep in mind when shopping—much more than a simple phrase like *Scandinavian minimalism* or *Parisian chic*. But it's also more useful. Putting in the time to think about where you stand on these factors will arm you for more efficient, less fraught decision-making, both online and in stores. It can be helpful to keep your answers to the following quiz handy, whether as a crib sheet in your wallet or a screenshot on your phone. That way, the next time you see a table, lamp, or pillow you think you love, you can consider it in the context of what you really want in your home. Eye on the prize, right?

INTERIOR DESIGNERS:

FRIEND OR FOE?

You might think that I'm anti–interior designer based on the title of this book or the fact that I'm advocating so hard for everyone to step up and be his or her own personal home stylist. That's not the case. True interior design is a métier for which I have intense admiration; interior designers are an incomparable source of inspiration, expertise, efficiency, and service. Trained, degreed interior designers have spent countless hours studying space planning, color theory, material science, and the psychology of space. They can speak to architecture and historic authenticity, and they can completely remake the look, feel, and function of a home. They know how and where to move walls, for Pete's sake!

But just like the culinary world has chefs, it also has home cooks. They serve very different clienteles, and their services require very different budgets. They have different tools at their disposal. Most people don't need or want their dinner cooked by a chef every night, but some people do—either they're busy, they're overwhelmed, they can afford it, or they just really like how that particular chef's food tastes. A lot of people enjoy having some of their meals plated by a professional toque and others slopped down with love by a spaghetti-slinging grandma. Different occasions. Different costs. Different circumstances.

This is to say that there's no "better" or "worse" between having a professionally designed interior and creating a self-styled home. And there's no reason to feel intimidated or self-conscious about interior design. So if picking up a high-end home magazine or shopping in an upscale furniture store makes you feel inadequate, stop. Stop going there, stop feeling that way. There are no rights or wrongs in interior design. Just as there's "Oh my God, this tuna tartare with yuzu emulsion is to die for," there's also "Oh my Lord, can I have your apple pie recipe." And just as most chefs didn't grow up eating béarnaise sauce every night, most designers had normal, comforting homes like yours. Read their books if you want to. Bookmark pictures of their work online. If you like their portfolio and can afford their services, hire them. But don't stress about how you measure up to or why you can't afford the pros. As a wise Internet meme once told me, you do you.

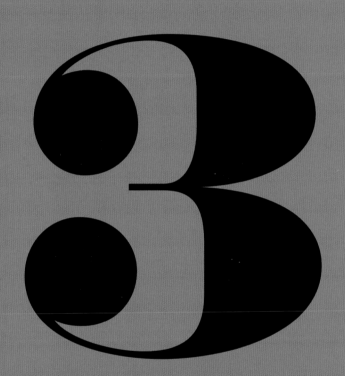

CHAPTER

3

CLEARING A PATH

GETTING RID OF WHAT DOESN'T WORK

Now that you know something about your personality and your design leanings, you need to make sure there's enough physical space for the stylish, functional, and personal elements you'd like to see in your home. And that means determining which of your own belongings, well, belong.

What does that mean, exactly? For starters, most room designs don't begin with a blank slate, even if you're moving into a brand-new, empty house. Our homes come with baggage, including but not limited to:

- Items we've made investments in and feel obligated to keep

- Items we've inherited from family or friends and feel guilty about shedding

- Pieces we think we're supposed to have, whether or not they jibe with our style (or lifestyle)

- Items we like that are functional but won't work for the space

- Items we like that are functional but do work for the space

This chapter is dedicated almost entirely to letting go of everything in every category but the last one (things you like that work as they should and work for the space). Why? Everything else prevents us from bringing home the items and furniture that reflect us and suit our real lifestyles.

The Struggle Is Real

My colleague Keriann struggled long and hard with a decision we're now calling the Teal Sofa Situation. Moving into a new apartment in a new city, she was pressed to furnish her house in a hurry (and on a tight budget), so she welcomed the donation of a dusty marine-hued love seat from her mother. It was a place to sit while she got acquainted with her new neighborhood, and it kept her from having to eat her takeout on the floor—not a bad score.

Eventually, though, Keriann began to settle in, and she wanted to make the space feel more like her own. Over several months, she picked up a new coffee table, a funky light fixture, and an area rug. But as she continued to fill out her space, she found herself struggling with that plush blue-green sofa, which didn't align with feel of the rooms and furnishings she loved in photos. Its deep seat and overstuffed cushions felt *too* relaxed, which had the inverse effect of making her feel unsettled, and the tired upholstery made the room feel drab, despite all of her new purchases.

After months of unsuccessfully trying to find pillows and accents that would make the sofa work, Keriann bit the bullet. Together, we picked out a new love seat she adored. It suited the space better, worked with the rug she'd already bought, and suddenly made the whole room look more elevated and chic.

The obvious question, of course, is one of cost. When funds are limited, why spend needed money on a new piece when something you currently have fits the bill on function? As Keriann wrestled with the decision to shell out, I encouraged her to think less about the line items and more about overall value—the value of feeling connected to the space. "If you loved your apartment, if it really felt like your perfect little nest, and if it looked like one of the pictures you've saved online, how long do you think you'd stay there?" I asked her.

"Indefinitely," she replied.

"What if you left it exactly as it is today? How soon do you think you'd consider moving?"

"Maybe at the end of my lease," she said. "I'm not sure."

My point: Moving is expensive. Security deposits are expensive. Going out all the time because you don't feel at home in your home is expensive. A new piece of furniture, then, is often less costly than it seems.

↑ Vetting your home's decor includes light fixtures. Just because your house came with a contractor-grade pendant doesn't mean you can't swap it for a glittering chandelier that's more your speed.

WHEN MAKING IT WORK
DOESN'T WORK

I'm all for small tweaks to help bring disparate parts of a room together. A coat of paint or a throw blanket can change the entire aesthetic of a piece and marry it with the other colors and styles in the home. But sometimes a piece doesn't merit the effort because it isn't "you."

Imagine, for a moment, that you're the type of person who always wears perfectly fitted skinny jeans. One day, you're on vacation and lose your luggage, and your host lends you a pair of overalls. You're grateful, sure, and you're comfortable. They're overalls, after all! And it's not like you can go outside without clothes on. But you don't necessarily feel like yourself in your borrowed attire. You consider styling the overalls so they look more "you"—maybe there's a cute jacket you could layer on top, you think, or a way to belt them to look more fitted. But those fixes cost money—money you wouldn't spend if you just sucked it up and bought another pair of perfectly fitted skinny jeans. The bottom line is, stop trying to convince yourself that your overalls are jeans. Get the piece you need before you waste any more time or money on the things you don't.

So what happened to Keriann's old teal sofa? She listed it online for $100, selling it to a happy apartment dweller and thus offsetting the cost of her pretty new velvet love seat. It was picked up the day the love seat was to be delivered. The sale was an exercise in good furniture karma—a way to keep the cycle going for another new-apartment dweller with nothing to sit on.

◀◀ When you mix in a wide variety of textures and shapes, neutral decor is far from boring. Incorporating a wood-slab table, knit ottoman, and chunky jute rug into this reading nook gives the space layers of interest.

In with the New, Out with the Old?

Whether you purge your unwanted things after or before you've found their replacements is entirely up to you and your design disposition. For some people, a blank space in their home—I'm looking at you, Pragmatists—is exactly the kind of kick start you need to find and buy a piece you love, lest your practical side ("But I already have a coffee table!") keep you from making the necessary move. Pull off the Band-Aid and dispose of that hand-me-down you hate. Dream Weavers also need a blank slate in order to create their room's new look.

Tinkerers will have less of an issue bringing in a new piece first, as they embrace the constant evolution of a room and they're likely to already have a new home planned for the old piece (even if that home is the classifieds). Self-Expressionists also tend to latch on to new items easily, as they're always on the lookout for pieces that feel very "them" and less emotionally tethered to items that don't.

Historians have the hardest time parting ways with their furniture. These folks usually fare best if they bring in the new piece first. That allows time to attach to the new look and feel of the room before trying to kick the old stuff to the literal curb. It also helps if the new piece has its own unique history or provenance, as it'll enrich the dialogue between items in the room. Move the ousted piece to an unused room, a garage, a shed, or the like, and put a Post-it on it dated for one month away. If you haven't found a great new spot for that piece elsewhere in your home by that date, it's time to put it up for adoption by a friend, donate it to a worthy organization, or list it for sale.

SIX WAYS TO

GET RID OF THINGS

1

Move them to a guest room or playroom, permanently or temporarily, if they work for that space.

Give them to a friend.

List them for sale online— think Craigslist, eBay, or consignment websites like Chairish.

4

Sell them via consignment stores.

5

Donate them to Goodwill. (Hello, tax write-off!)

6

Stick 'em on the curb with a "free" sign if you live in a city.

It's funny, I wasn't always such a huge proponent of selling or giving things away. Growing up, my mother was a Historian and Tinkerer, which meant she was attached to everything and could never get rid of anything—she'd just find a new place for it. "That's a good couch!" she'd exclaim to my sister regarding the sofa bed with no functioning springs left, as she rushed to the fabric store so she could reupholster it for a guest room.

The day I realized I could get rid of things and not have the waste gods smite me in my sleep was liberating. I started small with a knotty pine wine rack. My then-boyfriend (now husband) found the piece in our first apartment building, abandoned by a neighbor in the stairwell, and happily claimed it for our loft. Seven years and three moves later, it had taken up residence in our townhouse's dining room, where it stood in a corner and kept us from walking comfortably around the table. A friend, whose style is more rustic and casual (and who also happens to love wine), admired it as we sat down to dinner one night. "Take it!" I blurted out. "We don't really need it anymore."

"Really?" she asked. "I'd love something like this for a nook in my new house!" The day she took it out of my home, I felt great.

From then on, I was hooked. Mid-renovation, we moved a ton of stored furniture out into the yard while walls and plumbing were being replaced. That included a cast-iron bed that my husband had found in his grandmother's barn, shipped across three states, and refinished by hand. It was great when we had a full-sized bed, but we had upgraded to a king years before. "Jimmy!" I called to my carpenter. "Want an iron bed?" He happily took it away. And I have never looked back.

Replacing your decor with something cohesive doesn't have to be a pricey project. On this shelf, which floats above a bed, are a framed scrap of ticking-stripe fabric, a framed botanical print, dried eucalyptus, and a $20 leather tassel garland.

THE TOP FIVE

REASONS YOU'RE

HANGING ON TO YOUR STUFF

YOU LOVED IT WHEN YOU BOUGHT IT.

If you liked it then, shouldn't
you like it now?

YOU'RE SUFFERING FROM INERTIA.

It's here. It works. Why change?

IT BRINGS BACK GOOD MEMORIES.

Remember that party when
everyone sat around this table, sofa,
or kitchen island?

**REPLACING FURNITURE
SEEMS UNNECESSARILY EXPENSIVE.**

There are better things
to spend money on, right?

**YOU'RE UNSURE ABOUT WHAT
TO REPLACE IT WITH.**

Who's to say the next
piece will be any better?

THE TOP FIVE

REASONS TO

GET RID OF YOUR STUFF

YOU CAN SEE YOUR ROOM WITH FRESH EYES.

Imagine a new floor plan or color scheme without
the burden of belongings you don't like.

IT CAN SAVE YOU TIME.

Shopping for a fresh assortment of
furniture can be easier than shoehorning items
in to fit with what you have.

YOU GET A CLEAN START.

We often don't realize how grubby
or worn our old pieces are until we start shopping
for something new.

IT CAN SAVE YOU MONEY.

Replacing a piece with something
better for your life and style can be cheaper than
trying to dress up a bad purchase.

IT CAN MAKE YOUR HOME FEEL LARGER.

When your furnishings make you feel good and
enhance your home's flow, you end up with more
rooms you actually want to spend time in.

Arranged simply, natural decorative elements—a wood slice, palm leaves clipped from the garden, crackled porcelain, and a strand of meditation beads—make a mellow statement.

CHAPTER

4

WHERE PERSONALITY
MEETS REALITY

MAKING YOUR LOOK WORK FOR YOUR LIFESTYLE

PREVIOUS SPREAD: The only limit to your creativity with coffee-table decor is size—anything small enough works. This homeowner's display includes both the useful (playing cards, books, coasters) and the whimsical (an animal figurine). **OPPOSITE:** Balance, not symmetry, makes this mantel display feel intentional. A duo of weighty candlesticks is balanced on the opposite side by a tall, wide spray of leaves.

O nce you've taken a step back to understand your personal design makeup and cleared enough room in your home (and head) to start creating great spaces, it's time to shop, plan, design, and let your surroundings evolve. Your design disposition will absolutely inform how to tackle that process, but how?

Assuming every space in your home is ripe for a redo, here's what the process should *not* look like:

- Pinning pictures from the Internet into one giant pit of inspiration that you have no idea how to navigate and draw from as a shopper

- Going to the most expensive store in town and lamenting why you can't have it all

- Teaching yourself how to sew, upholster, hang wallpaper, tile, plumb, or wire new outlets

- Tearing apart the biggest (or nearest) room in your house

- Weeping every time you make a purchase that doesn't work out perfectly

These are universal don'ts. The do's—the where, how, and when of your decorating journey—will vary from person to person, and that's where your design disposition comes in.

How Disposition Dictates Design

In Chapter 1, we determined your design disposition(s). Now let's explore the pitfalls that plague design lovers of your ilk and the decorating do's that will serve you best in the long run.

Let's say you're a **SELF-EXPRESSIONIST.** You have no trouble expressing your tastes and can get attached to things you've accumulated over time, but the hardest part about pulling a look together is making all of the disparate pieces fit. Maybe you were a champion horseback rider and love nods to equestrian style, but you also spent a semester in Argentina and want reminders of that time in your home. How on earth do you make that all work?

Your focus should be on creating cohesion—finding the common threads in all of your disparate favorites and putting those elements at the core of your design. In the food world, you might create Thai-Mexican fusion by focusing on shared ingredients like mango, cilantro, and lime. The same goes for that riding champ—stucco whites and rich cognac leather might be just the things to pull it all together as one.

As for which makeover a **SELF-EXPRESSIONIST** should attempt first, is it tearing up that laundry room with the 1980s floral chintz border? I'd say no. While I'm all for quick fixes to make those hated spaces more tolerable (peel-and-stick wallpaper, anyone?), until you can really do them right, you're better off making your first big-time, big-money project a space that will feed your desire to make a personal statement. If your dream-home fantasy involves walking friends and guests into a space full of interesting conversation pieces, start with the sitting and dining rooms, which are places where you can really let loose. Between coffee tables, mantels, shelves, and walls, there are lots of surfaces where you can play with accents, colors, and textures.

Remember that decorating is a PROCESS, not always a perfectly PAVED PATH.

◀◀ A bamboo-inspired brass-and-mirror tray corrals smaller items on a polished wood table and is easily lifted away if the table needs to be used for cards or cocktails.

What if you're a **PRAGMATIST?** You adore efficient, purposeful, and, most important, finished spaces with no lingering to-dos. You want to plan your purchases well in advance, but you tend to plan spatially or financially rather than visually. At the same time, you loathe making mistakes, so you tend to not buy unless you're 100 percent sure about a piece, which you rarely are.

Your focus will be on surrendering to your style, teaching yourself to recognize on sight what works with your other stuff, and making a plan from there. Maybe you find the item and wait to buy it until your budget allows. But at least you'll be working style-first, which will get you closer to your dream space than filling in the room with whatever is priced well and ready to ship at the time you're ready to buy.

Where does a Pragmatist begin? You might spend the most energy on the kitchen, mudroom, and other get-'er-done spaces in the house. Unless you're starting over via a gut renovation, bringing personal style to these rooms typically requires less complete concept building, because there's less to customize. You're not typically dealing with floor-to-ceiling window treatments, upholstered furniture, or wall art, but rather adding personal flourishes to the foundations that currently exist.

HISTORIANS, meanwhile, have no trouble falling for a piece's unique shape, style, and story. Their biggest hurdles are knowing when to let go of excess furniture and decor, as they're sentimental about their things, and they can have trouble buying the "filler" furniture they need to make a room functional, not just interesting. They can also find mixing furniture styles challenging, as they tend to grow deeply enamored of specific design eras.

If this sounds like you, your focus should be on assessing the usefulness, not just the craftsmanship and provenance, of every item you own or think about bringing home. You'll need to learn how to mix older items with new items that elevate the presence of the things you prize (like cabinetry with glass windows or floating shelves for a collection of small antiques).

Historians are going to have an easier time starting in front-and-center spaces where period pieces are readily available and truly set the tone, like dining and living rooms. It's harder to make a midcentury or Victorian style statement in an office or powder room tucked in the back corner. Your style can and should creep into those spaces, but they're harder places to establish a look and feel for your whole home.

➥ A quirky mix of colorful tribal-inspired pillows and a vintage Oriental rug lend a lively, bohemian vibe to a neutral guest bedroom.

DREAM WEAVERS want their home to be an enveloping, mood-lifting retreat and for the experience of coming home to feel a little like visiting a hotel, entering an artfully designed restaurant, heading into a spa, or walking into the pages of a favorite catalog. Since Dream Weavers rarely want to sacrifice that experience over a price tag, sticking to a budget can be a concern. They also tend to get frustrated when they don't find the exact piece they think a room needs because they've fallen in love with it in a picture.

If you fall into this group, you'll benefit from the deep study of the room images you truly aspire to. What colors and materials show up often? What settings do the images evoke? Do they feel relaxed, exotic, or energetic? Often you can replicate the feel of a space with an entirely different set of furnishings—the key is capturing the personality rather than replicating others' designs piece for piece.

Dream Weavers might consider first tackling the entryway, a space that will greet you every day and that influences how you feel when you get home. A bedroom, master bath, or living room are also great places to start, as they're spaces where you go to relax and refresh.

The last group, the **TINKERERS,** treat decorating as a sport. They have no trouble buying items on a whim, and they're not bad at putting them together, either. But they can second-guess themselves, and it's a challenge for them to settle down and enjoy their home rather than messing with it constantly—to see real-life beauty and not tinker their way to the nuthouse (or poorhouse).

If you are a Tinkerer, focus on finishing rooms and letting them be. And once you've finished a room, indulge your habit with seasonal, affordable swaps like pillows, florals, and linens while letting your big purchases stay put.

As for where to start, Tinkerers can pick up just about anywhere, because they never really start or finish. Just begin with one or two of the big pieces that you truly need to replace—a rug for the dining room? A light for the hallway? Let the design spin out from your starting place, and you'll find yourself working (slowly, please!) on the adjacent rooms before you know it.

DESIGN
REVELATION
№ 2

Spaces have personalities

Different rooms can and should function differently, because you spend your time in them differently. That means you won't always build a room in the same way. Depending on what a room is used for, you might start with the seating, the tables, what's on the floor, the lighting, or what's on the walls. Start with the pieces that most influence the activity of the room and go from there.

◀◀ A couple counters their home's traditional New England architecture with a host of unconventional decor picks, from the oversize Audubon prints to the woven rattan pendant, flatweave rug, and sheepskin-draped farmhouse bench.

Starting Small

Whatever room you're in, I always recommend starting with one fixture item that you intend to keep and making small style tweaks to get yourself comfortable with the new process. Say you're a Pragmatist, and you know you eventually want a spruced-up kitchen. You might take something you like, such as your kitchen table, and change one small element about it, such as the table linens or the pendant light above. If you're a Historian, try reorganizing the vintage bookshelves or reframing the art on your walls. Just as a kid starting a new instrument will gain confidence if she can learn a simple song in the first few lessons rather than pounding away at chords for six months, you will get tons of satisfaction and build momentum by tackling projects you can complete and be happy with fast.

As you build on your early success and start redoing larger spaces, stay focused on the room at hand. If you find things you like for other spaces along the way, fabulous! Put them in "holding" room mock-ups (I'll get to this in Chapter 5) that you're not working on as actively, so you can come back to them later. Note: This doesn't apply if you find them in a you'd-be-a-moron-to-pass-this-up sale, in which case you should buy them and be fully prepared to have to work around those must-include pieces down the road. If you change your mind about them later, woohoo! You get to sell them, probably for more than you paid. Remember that it's a process—not always a perfectly paved path.

Storage does double duty as decor in this
space above a bedroom dresser, where hooks
and horns serve as jewelry hangers.

Keeping It Real

Before we can get to working with that room mock-up, there's one other thing to consider: the limitations of your daily lifestyle. This is the part where the waiter at the fancy restaurant says, "Does anyone at the table have any food allergies?" Because this will affect the meal, er, home you're creating, and it's best to take it into account early before someone goes into anaphylactic shock or you discover that no, in fact, a black sofa and a white long-haired cat are not a match made in design heaven. So raise your hand if you have any of the following:

- Children
- Pets
- A spouse who dislikes throw pillows
- Narrow stairs, tight corners, or other furniture-delivery obstacles
- Roommates
- A landlord

These things matter because they stand to come between you and long-term happiness in your Pinterest dream home. But if you consider these issues when making your room mock-up, you're less likely to be blindsided with a "Man, that was dumb" moment of self-hatred when the sofa you ordered arrives and just doesn't work.

A friend of mine has a tiny condo in the city, and I mean *tiny*: the kitchen is practically the living room, which is practically the bedroom. So when shopping together for her home, we needed to consider that every piece could be seen from any angle, so different color schemes for different spaces were not an option, and every item needed to incorporate some element of utility or storage. At the same time, she craved serenity amid the cramped chaos. Everything needed to feel unified and cohesive, practical yet Zen all at once. With these limitations, she feared she'd never find pieces to make her tiny condo into a home.

DESIGN
REVELATION
№ 3

Pieces have personalities

Not all furniture and seating are created equal. Take sofas, for example. Depending on the fabric, cushioning, seat height, seat depth, and leg style, one eighty-inch gray sofa can be fabulous in a living room, and another eighty-inch gray sofa looks bizarre. Before you buy, ask the piece what it feels like (formal? funky? loungy?) and try to determine whether its character, not just its price and size, can be friendly with the rest of your room's cast.

◄◄ Like a luxe shag rug, a Mongolian lamb's wool pillow brings bold glamour and texture to a seating area, but with less commitment. If the pillow gets stained or damaged, replacing it won't totally break the bank—or upset the whole room's design.

It turned out to be easier than she anticipated. I think constraints can help us become better, more efficient shoppers. Just as a person with lactose intolerance quickly acclimates to scanning menus for butter, cream, and cheese, knowing your built-in "can't haves" will get you comfortable saying "It's nice, but not for me." That leaves you with more time to zero in on the things that could be for you, checking the dimensions, and testing them out in your room mock-up to be sure that they work. More chance at success. Fewer tummy aches. Win.

Here are some rules of thumb for dealing with the above constraints.

IF YOU HAVE CHILDREN

- **Think soft and round.** Avoid chairs with wooden arms jutting out into the walkway, tables with sharp corners, and table legs that stick out and beg to be tripped on.

- **Keep breakables up high.** You can still have nice things. They just have to remain out of reach until the kids are old enough to know what's fragile.

- **Consider stains.** Dark fabrics, easy-to-clean materials like wool and indoor/outdoor canvas, and stain-treated textiles are a no-brainer. Ivory linen that needs to be professionally cleaned? Think twice.

- **Anticipate wear.** Vintage pieces and already distressed items won't show marks like very formal, polished wood furniture, so they're excellent for kid-friendly homes.

- **Beware of tipping.** Top-heavy furniture that topples easily is a no-go in a home with kids. Choose tables and chairs that are more stable and will take the occasional bump with a soccer ball without falling over.

IF YOU HAVE PETS

- **Consider stains.** Even well-groomed pets can track dirt in on their paws, so pale rugs and upholstery should be purchased with extreme caution. Like parents of small humans, pet parents are better off outfitting their homes with easy-to-clean, durable materials like synthetic-blend fabrics or washable wool. Leave the silk and mohair to the folks without furry friends.

- **Consider camouflage.** It sounds silly, but if pet hair is your biggest concern, coordinating your upholstery with your animals can buy you a bit more time between brushing and vacuuming sessions. No one wants to be chasing a white dog off a navy armchair every five minutes because of the shedding, so taupe is a more practical pick.

IF YOUR SPOUSE IS LOATH TO FLUFF A PILLOW

- **Choose decor that looks good in disarray.** High-maintenance decor and impatient mates don't marry well. If your cohabitant won't tidy the cushions or keep the nesting tables arranged just so, you'll need to pick pieces that look as good partially styled as when they're perfectly arranged. A patterned headboard can provide fashionable pop, eliminating your need for piles of printed pillows; a Moroccan pouf you use as an ottoman looks just fine if it's left in the middle of the room. When picking items for your space, imagine the real-life scenarios and make sure your chosen pieces work for those moments as well.

- **Keep it simple.** The fewer decorative items to tweak and adjust with each cleaning, the less you'll get on each other's nerves. Go for big statement pieces instead of lots of small ones, as there's less to tinker with on a day-to-day basis.

If your dining room gets regular use, chairs upholstered in a durable, wipe-clean microfiber or an indoor/outdoor fabric (like Sunbrella) will be more stain-resistant than linen or velvet. If your family is especially mess-prone, skip the upholstered chairs altogether; there are non-fabric options in every style, from traditional wood to glam Lucite and modern molded plastic.

Just because a piece is designed for a certain function doesn't mean you can't use it where and how you like. A round wall clock leaned inside a bookcase helps to fill out an empty shelf, while a charming brass owl, once a vintage tea-light holder, helps keep it standing upright.

◀◀ If you have little ones, display breakables and items with sharp edges on high surfaces, such as tall windowsills and upper bookshelves. Stick to books, nontoxic plants, and other kid-safe items on coffee and end tables.

IF YOU LIVE IN TIGHT QUARTERS

- **Go modular.** Bunching tables are easier to get through small entries than large coffee tables. Floating wall shelves are easier to carry up narrow stairs than a six-tier étagère. Folding and stacking chairs are easier to move than dining armchairs. You get the picture.

IF YOU HAVE ROOMMATES

- **Go neutral.** Your furnishings are going to need to marry well with someone else's, so choose versatile materials such as neutral beige or gray upholstery and punch things up with pillows and throws. Don't overspend on anything in a common area, as others won't care for your custom upholstery as you would. The good stuff in a great hue goes in your own room. At the same time...

- **Be selfish.** Don't buy anything you don't personally love because it complements roommates' furniture. There's a good chance it will be coming with you when your shared lease is up, so it should work best with your own belongings, not theirs.

IF YOU HAVE A LANDLORD

- **Think removable.** Your decor shouldn't keep you from getting your security deposit back. That may mean mounting your curtain panels on tension rods instead of screwing them into the walls or choosing a peel-and-stick wallpaper instead of a pasted-back, permanent installation. Lighting might have to be plug-in versus hardwired.

- **Think movable.** Anything of value that you add to your home should be easy to take with you—lightweight, neutral, and flexible enough to work in a future home of unknown shape and size. Two storage cubes are more versatile than one storage bench at the end of the bed; two dining chairs that you might use in a future home office are a smarter buy than industrial-style dining stools that suit the apartment's built-in breakfast bar. Think ahead, and you'll be able to enjoy the pieces you purchase for many years—and in many homes—to come.

Whatever your design challenges—mental or physical—resist the urge to think of them as horrible, confining limitations on your creativity. They're not constraints, they're guardrails to keep your choices on track, and they'll help steer you efficiently toward things that work. Paying attention is paying it forward. With clear criteria for your perfect furnishings in mind, you'll be on the fast track to a space you love in real life, and putting the pieces together will be easier than you imagined.

FROM PIN TO PLAN

CREATING A ROOM MOCK-UP

PREVIOUS SPREAD: Not sure if a shaggy Moroccan-style rug will work with a rustic dining table or blond wood chairs? A room mock-up can help you play with material mixes before spending a dime. OPPOSITE: Mixing patterns, especially on similarly sized pillows, takes practice. Putting images together in a room mock-up can help you visualize how the small- and large-scale prints you're considering will look together in real life.

For a long time, one of the biggest obstacles to decorating your own home was the inability to keep all of your ideas in one accessible place. You could tear out magazine pages, sure, but then you might not have your trusty binder of photos with you when shopping, or even a clue how to utilize them if you did.

Then came the Internet, and suddenly everyone had a pinboard online and access to a million ideas and pictures they could easily bookmark. From cloud-based browsers to websites that let you access your saved images from anywhere, it's now easier than ever to gather, gather, gather, and then tap into your amassed trove of prettiness on the go.

But even with inspiration more accessible and portable than ever, what do you *do* with all that information? For most of us, the answer is nothing. The dream homes and looks we love continue to live online, and only online.

Beyond trying to convince you to start bringing home the pieces and looks you love, this chapter is one giant case for creating a room mock-up—a centralized destination where you can compile your product selections and view them in relation to one another. A room mock-up will serve as your decorating North Star—an indispensable guide that'll show you the way. I couldn't design a room without one.

Images of items you own and
want to keep (for now)

A swatch of the paint color

Images of key architectural
features or details in the room

Images of items you're
considering buying

Room Mock-Up Basics

At its simplest, a room mock-up is a virtual room you put together online—a safe place where you can try out new ideas without ever spending a dime. Whether you're starting with a totally bare space or your home is halfway to being featured on *Hoarders,* this living document is a tool you can refer to and rely upon throughout the decorating process.

Regardless of what program you use (see "Getting Technical," page 84), the process is the same. You'll start by populating the collage with images of items you own or are 90 percent sure you'll acquire. They can be pictures of the exact item, uploaded from your camera or phone, or you can do what I do and find a picture of something nearly identical (same shape, same finish, same proportions) on the Web and use that as a stand-in for the real thing. As much as possible, try to a use clean picture of the item you own: move it in front of a blank wall before snapping a pic, or crop the image to remove as much of the background decor as possible. This will help you imagine how the piece will live among other new items. On the side or in an additional document, record the dimensions of the room, including ceiling heights and window measurements—this will come in handy when deciding whether large pieces like sofas, tall mirrors, and area rugs will fit.

Once you have the bones of the room mock-up in place, you're ready to add in new items that pique your interest, trying them out to see how they look with everything that's already in your mock-up. Thinking the bedroom could use a bold yellow lamp? Pop one on the nightstand and see how it looks. Found a cool armchair on an auction site? Drag the image into your living room and see how it jibes with your sofa and coffee table.

How is a room mock-up different from a saved product list or a board of pinned images you find online? For starters, it lets you understand how the various pieces relate to one another. You can put throw pillows on a sofa to see how the fabrics really look together. You can enlarge or reduce the size of the coffee table so its ratio to the sofa is approximately correct. You can start to see things you might not notice in a product list or pinboard, like the fact that all of your colorful accents are on the left side of the room. You can determine how the new works with the old, or how exchanging one item for another can change the entire look of a space. As long as you update the board as your design comes together, you'll be surprised at how closely the room you've mocked up resembles the room you've created online.

➤➤ Putty-toned cabinetry, marble counters, rose-gold hardware, and dark basalt tile all coexist in this city kitchen.

➤ A room mock-up of the space at right shows how the various finishes—painted wood, dark stone tile, shiny chrome fixtures, an Oriental rug—would look together in real life.

➤ Don't just include your statement pieces—like this capiz (oyster-shell) chandelier—in your room mock-ups. Make sure you also include imagery of significant architectural features, such as these large wooden ceiling beams, as they also play into the overall look, feel, and color balance of the room.

Getting Technical

You don't have to be a tech genius or graphic designer (Lord knows I'm not) to create a really useful mock-up. Sure, you can make an A-plus, magazine-worthy version if you know how to use the program Adobe Illustrator, but I've seen great, highly useful room mock-ups created with basic software like Microsoft Excel.

At a minimum, you need to be able to add images to a document, crop them as needed, and shuffle the order of the images in the "stack"—that is, be able to move the pillow pictures to the front so they don't get hidden by the larger sofa picture.

Personally, I've been using Google Drawings for years, precisely because I'm not a graphic designer and because I get all flustered when I see the menu of brushes and image layers and all that jazz in the more advanced design tools. I like being able to just drag in pictures from websites or ones that I've saved on my computer's desktop. Bonus: It's free!

Of course, it's possible that 3-D room visualizers, which let you see proposed furnishings in your space, will totally be a thing by the time this book hits shelves. If not, they're coming soon, and we'll have an even greater ability to toy with our design ideas sans commitment. But I can't claim I won't still use my indispensable 2-D mock-ups.

➤ Just because a room is decorated in neutrals doesn't mean a room mock-up can't help you refine the design. It can ensure that your disparate finishes, like iron, painted wood, and granite, all work together for a cohesive look.

Mock-Up Do's and Don'ts

Speaking from experience, here are a few pieces of advice for building and using your room mock-ups.

- **Do take a screenshot of your mock-up every time you make major changes.** Save it to your phone or computer. Whether you see an item or idea you like while out shopping, while reading magazines, or while visiting a friend or dining in a hip restaurant, it's great to be able to look at your latest plan for the room and decide, on the spot, whether the newcomer is worth adding to your "might" list.

- **Don't assume you'll remember where you originally found a product or image.** I've dropped plenty of gorgeous pieces into mock-ups, only to forget the source and be unable to finally purchase them when the time came. Keep links to your contenders saved as bookmarks on your computer, or add a tiny text box next to the item in your mock-up. You'll thank yourself, I promise.

- **Do put your room mock-up to a personal-style test.** Remember all those style preferences you sussed out in Chapter 2? Before you act on anything, ask yourself whether the mocked-up room reflects your ultimate color tolerance, formality level, etc. It's easy to grow enamored of specific products you've placed in your mock-up while losing sight of your end goal for the space. For example, say you've fallen for some colorful pillows and built a great room design that incorporates them well, but the rooms you ultimately admire skew neutral. Taking a step back to ensure your design aligns with your big-picture preferences can help you avoid decorator's remorse.

- **Do keep measurements in mind.** It's easy to place a mirror above a table and think, Hey, that looks pretty good! But it's critical to note the measurements of your pieces when you put them in your mock-up and check any new additions to be sure you're creating a real-ish representation of the whole room—especially items that really need to work together. No one wants to end up ordering a coffee table that's two feet longer than the sofa (oops!) or a dining chair that leaves you with your chin on the table.

DESIGN
REVELATION
№ 4

It's all about proportion.

One of the benefits of having a room mock-up in addition to any pinboards or saved-item lists you have with retailers is being able to visualize the proportions of various colors, patterns, and materials in your room. One zebra-print chair can be funky, but eight of them around a dining table is a whole other level of wild. That's not something you can always glean from a product list. Buying eight chairs? Put eight of them in your mock-up. I guarantee it'll change how you see the space.

◄◄ Balance is the goal of every room and every room mock-up. This living room, centered around a brick-and-brass fireplace, could easily have looked heavy and dated. But thanks to white walls and bookshelves, leafy green plants, and a modern white rocking chair, the vibe is eclectic and collected.

TWO

STYLING

YOUR

HOME

SOCIAL SPACES

LIVING ROOMS, FAMILY ROOMS & DINING ROOMS

From starting your mock-up to picking out pillows and hanging artwork, knowing your design disposition will influence how you approach the process. But that doesn't mean there aren't universal truths about decorating, and that's what these next few chapters are all about. Whether you're a Self-Expressionist, Pragmatist, Historian, Dream Weaver, or Tinkerer, heeding this advice as you shop for, discover, and acquire pieces to fill your home will give you the best chance of long-term design success, no matter your personality or aesthetic.

Take, for starters, social spaces like living rooms, dining rooms, and sitting areas. These rooms are where we hang out with family, roommates, and friends—where we convene to talk about the good in our days, to grouse about the noisy neighbors, to share a cocktail (or three) and solve the world's problems. And yet they're so often the opposite of comfortable or comforting. People jockey for the seat with the best view; they struggle to find a spot to set their coffee mug. Unused chairs and tables get piled with throw pillows or magazines.

Other times, the spaces become rarely used showplaces, like the dressy parlor that's pretty but somehow uninviting or the formal dining room reserved for once-a-year meals. Instead of gathering in the rooms that are intended for socializing, everyone clusters in the kitchen. "That's where the action is," many say. But I think it's often the only space in the house where visitors can easily settle in—where no seat is better than another, where everyone finds a spot by the counter where their elbows fall at just the right height, and where there's always a convenient place to set a drink.

Why not design your social spaces to be as inviting as a kitchen full of simmering pots? It's not as hard as it sounds. A great social space will have three key components: plenty to look at; comfortable, well-placed seating; and tables exactly where you need them. You'll know you've mastered the mix when it's impossible to get guests off the sofa when it's time to eat, and when you can't seem to get your dinner guests to push back from their plates before midnight. The key is providing those features that encourage people to gather and linger, anticipating their needs while doing so.

PREVIOUS SPREAD: With a cool green chandelier, an oversize bowl filled with lemons, and mismatched wall art, an open dining space is anything but formal. OPPOSITE: A townhouse parlor, while small, feels airy and welcoming thanks to a Louis Philippe–style mirror that emphasizes the room's height and a glass coffee table that keeps sight lines clear.

Ease is everything in a living room anchored by a sectional sofa covered in a linen blend. Navy curtain panels, hung casually from clips, lend the space a laid-back vibe, while an upholstered ottoman beckons guests to put their feet up. A vintage chair, scored at an antiques fair, can be moved around the room as needed.

In a Boston townhouse, a couple's love of color and pattern is on display in the first-floor sitting area. An antique table and a brass floor lamp nod to this 1870 townhouse's history, while an eclectic mix of decor—vintage posters, a Moroccan-style pillow, a modern chevron pattern on the ottoman—offer unexpected freshness.

DESIGN **REVELATION** № 5

The more personal the space, the more personal the details should be.

I always find it a bit jarring to see enormous family or wedding portraits in a more public space, like a sitting room by the front door or a formal dining room. To me, those intimate moments are better shared in the deeper parts of a home, such as a hallway to the bedrooms or the bedrooms themselves. A social space can be so much more inviting and intriguing when it showcases the inhabitants' style and point of view instead of cataloging their awards, milestones, and intimate memories. If you have more than one living space, like a formal sitting room and a relaxed family room, think about containing the more personal stuff—the wedding-kiss close-up, the newborn shots, the framed gymnastics medal—to the more casual of the two rooms.

Who Thrives Here?

Naturally, social spaces are where Self-Expressionists, Historians, and Dream Weavers can really shine. These rooms usually offer lots of surface area for displaying objects of interest, like decorative antiques on the book-shelves or buffet. You can set books with intriguing titles on the coffee table and showcase framed photos and souvenirs on the console. And since these rooms are the spaces you're likely to sit in with guests (as opposed to, say, the master bedroom or mudroom), it makes a lot of sense for storytelling types like Self-Expressionists, Historians, and Dream Weavers to cluster their prized items here, rather than in a more functional or personal room that visitors will never see.

What that means is, barring any reasons to start elsewhere, social spaces are where these three design dispositions should focus their energies. Tinkerers, being more stop-and-go in their design process, can fold social spaces into any part of their plan. Pragmatists, meanwhile, may find these rooms frustrating or harder to master since there's so much mood-setting involved, so they might put off designing these rooms until they've finished other projects first. Once they're ready, however, the rules below will offer the framework they need to get started.

◀◀ In the dining room of a Spanish-style California house, it's all about visual balance. While the hefty beamed ceiling draws the eye up, the other elements—a cascading shell chandelier, a weighty trestle-style table, and tall floor mirrors—help to keep the focus at eye level.

▶▶ Combining the homeowners' love for sleek, Eastern-inspired decor with a bit of glamour and a dash of surf style, a San Diego–area great room fits its residents to a T.

Where to Begin

This may seem counterintuitive, but if you have the luxury of starting from scratch, shop for and put rug(s) into your room mock-up along with other fixture items (say, the $2,000 sofa you already bought last year) before you start filling out the design with anything new. Why go from the ground up? For one thing, amply sized, high-quality rugs can be an investment, and it's preferable to know how much you'll need to set aside for the piece you want. Second, rugs "touch" every part of the space. If you try to bring in a patterned rug after you've chosen throw pillows, colorful side chairs, wall art, and curtains, you may find yourself struggling to make it all work. Start with your rug, on the other hand, and you'll be able to incorporate those smaller purchases with a cohesive end result in mind.

Rugs aside, the most defining piece in a social space is the seating, so consider it next. Do not—I repeat, do not—simply go to your local furniture showroom, even if it has door-buster deals and a discotheque inside, and buy the first matching sofa–love seat–chair combo or dining table–chair–buffet set that catches your eye. Even if you're a Pragmatist and you appreciate the efficiency of furnishing a room in one fell swoop, I'll give you three good reasons to MIY (mix it yourself) your furniture combination:

- **Nailing the dimensions.** Every room has its own unique layout and details that should influence the furniture choices, from the position of the fireplace to the height of the windows to the location of the doorways. Pre-matched seating and dining groups will rarely suit the room in a natural, appealing way.

- **Visual appeal.** There are certainly exceptions, but matched seating sets are rarely the height of design. They tend to be oversized, overstuffed, and feature weird, doctor's office–type fabrics and prints. Likewise, the dining room–in–a–box can make a room feel one-note and deny you some interesting design opportunities, like mixing upholstered seating with a wood table and a great metal wine rack. Create your own combination, and you'll be rewarded with a far more dynamic room.

- **Flexibility.** A matched set can quickly overwhelm a space and force every other design choice to accommodate its look, which helps no one in the long term. Pragmatists in particular will hate having to redo or replace the entire set when one piece gets damaged, and Tinkerers will hate being bound by one element of the design. If you combine pieces from different sources and collections, you'll have an easier time swapping out or replacing individual items as they wear out (or as you tire of them).

The more dramatic the piece, the earlier it should factor into the design.

Generally speaking, the more fixture furnishings you already have designated for the space, the more neutral you'll need the filler pieces to be. If a fabulous, attention-getting rug is your thing, pick it out first and aim to make your subsequent additions supporting cast rather than dueling divas. This will help ensure everything layers together harmoniously down the road and your picks aren't fighting for eyes.

Room-Planning Guidelines

Combining disparate sofas, sectionals, love seats, and accent chairs can sound daunting, but the process will be easier if you keep the following rules of thumb in mind:

- **Think in scenes.** When people are hanging out in this space, do you expect them to be clustered in one group or spread around the room doing different things and having separate conversations? Furnish to support those scenarios: If it's one big, jovial conversation you're after, bigger pieces like sectionals and long sofas, plus big coffee tables flanked with chairs facing the sofa, are a better idea than many smaller armchairs spread across the room. If the room might simultaneously contain TV watchers, newspaper readers, or homework doers, you'll want more smaller pieces that you can cluster up to create distinct, intimate conversation zones away from one another. If you want the space to be flexible, consider incorporating movable seating, such as upholstered ottomans, poufs, benches, or lightweight side chairs, into your room's mix, so that guests can create their own impromptu seating groups. The more scenarios you account for, the more likely you are to use the room.

- **Pay attention to distance.** Whether there's one hangout area in a room or five, allow at least twenty-four inches of clearance, preferably thirty-six inches, anywhere you expect folks to walk. Another important consideration is whether these paths (from one hangout space to another or to exit the room) are straight lines or circumnavigate furniture and corners. Keep the traffic flow as clear as possible to avoid creating a room that leaves its inhabitants feeling trapped.

If the idea of painting a room a dark hue, like this navy dining room, is intimidating, placing a swatch of your chosen shade in a room mock-up can allay your fears. Here, the walls are balanced by white wainscoting, white ceilings, and a white linen chandelier shade.

After choosing a bold Scalamandré wallpaper and hand-painting a checkerboard pattern on the floors, this dining room's owner chose clear Ghost chairs and a Venetian-glass chandelier that would suit the room's level of glamour without stealing the show.

DESIGN
REVELATION
Nº 7

Sometimes you need to pretend.

A professional designer might be able to tell offhand whether a sofa or rug is the right size for a room, but for the rest of us, some pre-purchase pantomiming can help. If you're in the market for a coffee table, sit on the sofa and mime setting down your drink, putting up your feet, and other normal living room activities, then measure the height of your imaginary table to determine the ideal height. Likewise, try reaching to turn on a lamp you have yet to buy—would you be able to switch it on from where you're sitting? Props can also be helpful. Place a flipped-over box (or several) where you're thinking of putting a piece of furniture to see how it changes the balance of a room. If you're contemplating an eight-by-ten-foot rug, outline it in painter's tape on the floor so you can see what it covers. Hang cardboard on an empty wall before you splurge on art. Practice means less risk—and a whole lot more reward.

• **"Weigh" your furniture.** Imagining that each piece has a certain weight will help you create balance within each conversation area in the room (and make the group feel like it makes sense in the larger space). The wider, taller, darker, and more patterned a piece of furniture, the more weight you should assign to it; backless benches and leggy chairs tend to feel lighter. Instead of thinking something is "too big" or "too small" for the room, shift to thinking about an item's overall dominance and its proportion to everything else in the space. A thick-lined concrete coffee table might not feel heavy at all if it's placed in the center of a seating group. Looking at the room as a whole, assess whether it's evenly weighted from one side to another and make adjustments, like choosing a heftier piece or adding some bold, thickly framed art to that side of the room to counteract the visual imbalance.

- **Don't fear the float.** There's a natural tendency to line the walls with seating. (Think of every college apartment in the history of man, in which a futon lines one side of the room, the TV is on the opposite wall, and a dinky coffee table sits in the middle. There's usually a recliner on an angle off to the side, which ends up being everyone's favorite seat.) Similarly, sectionals are often placed reflexively into the corner, simply because they're corner-shaped. But upholstery shouldn't simply fill corners in a room; it should tell people where to sit down and how to use each part of a room. One leg of a sectional hanging freely in a room can create a visual boundary, for example, separating a TV-watching area from a reading nook. Two chairs nestled together facing a bay window, with their backs to the rest of the room, can make that zone feel like a destination for quiet conversation rather than an awkward outcropping.

- **Take tables seriously.** Just because they're not soft doesn't mean they don't make a room more comfortable. Well-sized, well-placed tables complete a space and make it feel truly livable. Whether it's a coffee table that's just an arm's distance from the sofa or an end table that puts a table lamp at just the right height for reading, they provide comfort and ease. Tables can also help ground other items in the room, such as a sofa that's floating freely in front of a fireplace. Flank that sofa with two lamp tables and back it with a narrow console (aka a sofa table), and suddenly it's a visual boundary that transforms one large space into two distinct rooms.

In the living room of a renovated Tudor, a pair of spare dining chairs find a second home by the window (and bring a boost of room-awakening color). A set of L-shaped corner chairs placed side by side almost read as an opposing sofa, helping to define the conversation area within the room.

➤➤ An unfussy mix of patterned pillows livens up a simple gray sofa, while unexpected decor pieces like a vintage mirror and mismatched pottery create a homey, relaxed air.

↑ Four quirky alcoves in a townhouse ceiling become a focal point after the addition of vintage metal letters.

Here are a few ideas for underused arrangements you can incorporate into your living room or sitting room floor plan. For larger spaces, you can either increase the dimensions of each piece (choosing extra-deep seating, for example, or an extra-long sofa) or carve the room into more conversation areas using a wider variety of the combinations below. It all depends on how you want the room to be used, not to mention your budget and interest in designing several spaces within a space.

THE FACE-OFF
Two sofas facing each other. Ideal for sitting rooms with an ambient focal point, like a fireplace or artwork (not a TV).

THE CONVERSATION CORNER
Two matching or similarly proportioned chairs set on an angle, with a martini table or lamp table in between. Ideal for bay windows, corners of a room, and creating a conversation area set off from the main conversation group.

THE BACK-TO-BACK
Two sofas facing in opposite directions, each furnished with its own coffee table. Ideal for extra-large rooms that you'd like to divide into two distinct spaces, such as one facing the TV and another for socializing separately.

THE SISTER SEATS
Two matching accent chairs placed side by side opposite or catty-corner to a sofa. Ideal for more formal spaces where guests might not want to sit right next to one another on a sofa, or where you'd rather not block airflow with a larger piece.

◀◀ Despite its wide mix of materials and tight proportions, this dining room feels airy and welcoming. The key? A neutral palette, open-back chairs, and plenty of glass. (Note the chandelier, framed art, and china cabinet.)

As for the dining room, these are some of my favorite ways to deviate from the standard matching-chairs-around-a-table arrangement.

THE BENCH-MADE

A long, backless bench replaces the side chairs on one side of the table. Ideal for dining areas that open to another space, as the lower profile of the bench keeps the two areas from feeling divided.

THE BIG BANQUETTE

Another high–low arrangement, this setup puts an upholstered, armless banquette on one side and low benches or stools that can be tucked under the table on the opposite side. Ideal for a small dining space, like a breakfast nook, where you can save room by putting the banquette flush against the wall.

THE EAST–WEST WING

Instead of the standard-issue armchairs that come with a dining set, try two grand wing chairs instead—just check the seat and arm heights to ensure the folks sitting in them are positioned comfortably for dining rather than lounging. Ideal for big rooms with tall ceilings or anywhere you want to make a dramatic statement, such as a more formal dining room.

FIVE WAYS TO STYLE A COFFEE TABLE

People have a wide range of tolerance for coffee-table decor. Some love the chance to create a little moment in a social space, while others think the surface is best used for, well, coffee. Whether your tastes lean minimal or maximal, one of these five approaches to styling one of your home's frequently used surfaces will likely suit you.

1

THE BOOKWORM

Stacks of coffee-table books nearly cover this table's surface, begging to be picked up and read. To keep the arrangement from looking like a bookstore display, mix in personal details with varied shapes and colors, such as flowers and round coasters, and set a few of the topmost books at an angle.

BEST FOR:
Self-Expressionists, Tinkerers

2

THE FLORIST

A bold bunch of blooms is the star of this coffee-table display, and everything else—a book or two, a simple bowl—plays second fiddle. Go big for maximum impact, either by clustering several bunches of flowers tightly in a large vase as shown, or by choosing taller branching florals that reach up and out.

BEST FOR: Dream Weavers

3

THE SHAPE-SHIFTER

If your coffee table is really an upholstered ottoman, top it with a large tray or, better yet, two nested trays, which you can dress up with accents, use for drinks, or remove when you're in the mood to put your feet up. Here, a shapely succulent adds a pop of brightness, a gold candle lends an exotic aroma, and a handful of collected shells provide a bit of organic charm.

BEST FOR: Pragmatists

4

THE MUSEUM

All manner of decor finds a home on this coffee table: pretty books, plants, a tray, ceramic objects, and more. To keep the mix feeling purposeful and balanced rather than haphazard, vary the heights of the items on display, and repeat shapes and colors (like the ceramic flowers or the gold finish on both the round tray and the glass box) more than once.

BEST FOR: Tinkerers, Historians

5

THE BASICS

A book, some coasters, and one decorative object are all it takes to make a glass table feel dressed. If your coffee table is usually topped with remote controls, consider placing them in a round basket, tray, or bowl to keep them neatly within reach.

BEST FOR: Pragmatists

> **TIP** ➡ *When selecting a coffee table, take cues from both the furniture and how people will move around the room. Generally speaking, round tables look and function best with sectionals, rectangular or oval tables look best in front of traditional sofas, and square tables are ideal when you have a large room and seating on multiple sides of the table.*

There's no rule saying your decor has to match the style of your home. In this midcentury split-level, contemporary seating mingles with an organic driftwood table and a leather shag rug; jewel-toned cushions and a cozy knit pouf provide pops of modern color.

Character Assessments

As you seek out pieces to fill each slot in your plan, do your best to think in 3-D, considering not just each piece's proportions, but also its personality. Here's how:

Aim for a mix of shapes. Even in the starkest, most modernist of spaces, it's nice to balance out sharp lines and corners with the occasional round or curvaceous piece. An oval coffee table can temper the harshness of a track-armed midcentury sofa, while a pillowy armchair might benefit from the structure of a blocky table by its side. I like to balance tall wingback chairs with short tub chairs on the opposite side of the room and pair lower-profile chesterfield sofas with high-backed balloon chairs for quirkiness and drama.

Combine high and low with care. Speaking of height, note that the higher the seat back of a chair or sofa, the less the piece will integrate with whatever's behind it. That means high-backed chairs can be great for defining separate areas of a room, but they can also keep folks from mingling. As you select furniture for a social space, be cognizant of how you want people and chitchat to travel across a room, and make sure the pieces foster the interactions you're after.

Dictate formality in subtle ways. An accent chair might seem like an accent chair, but I firmly believe that the details of different pieces give off subliminal mood cues, and choosing your pieces purposefully can help you set your room's tone. Simply speaking, leggy, tightly upholstered furniture tends to look more formal and less comfortable than skirted furniture, and slipcovered pieces are more casual still. The softer and more washable-looking the fabric, the more easygoing the room will look.

Decor and flower arrangements with some height, like this bowl of gently curving phalaenopsis orchids, can help to draw the eye up and make a room feel taller.

An event planner and her family inhabit this decor-filled living room. While every nook is filled, it's "happy clutter": a carefully selected mix of meaningful pieces that together create a narrative about their tastes and life.

Seat depths and seat cushioning can also influence the perception of a room. Deeper, lower, and cushier seats force you to recline and relax, which makes them fabulous for lounging and movie watching, but they may not be right for a room where you plan to host neighbors and coworkers for coffee or cocktails. (Imagine rising elegantly from a low-slung sofa in a pencil skirt or suit—it's just not possible.) Similarly, velvet or linen upholstery may be lovely in a reading or sitting room but a horror in a living room where kids down cereal and greasy chips while watching TV. In the latter scenario, you're far better off with an easy-care fabric such as a Sunbrella one, a wool blend, or a stain-treated cotton. If you pick your seating based on its mood and use as well as its looks, you'll be far more likely to use the room as you originally intended.

In the Details

Little things like windows, lighting, artwork, and accents can make the biggest difference in whether a room is perceived to be a hangout space, an elegant escape, or a place to be avoided. They're tone-setters, not accessories, so pay them their due.

WINDOWS

Don't underestimate the power of window treatments to set a living or dining room's tone. Pick your curtains and shades based on more than just color and print. Personality matters, too. Are they loose and casual or pleated and tailored? Which fits better with your room's look? Most importantly, are your curtain panels sized to fit the space? Excepting any soaring thirty-foot ceilings, window treatments look best when mounted as high above the windows as possible, and the wider you can set them (open curtains should ideally land outside the window frame), the larger your windows will look and the more light you'll let in the room.

A sofa placed in the center of this long, narrow room helps define two separate zones. In front of the sofa, guests gather for coffee and conversation; behind it, there's a table and benches for dining and homework.

LIGHTS

Unless you're using your living or dining room as a laboratory, you'll want far more than just recessed ceiling lights to illuminate your room. Aim for a variety of fixtures, ideally on dimmer switches, that allow you to set lots of different moods with light throughout the day. Consider incorporating any combination of sconces (hardwired or plug-in), picture lights, pendants, floor lamps, and table lamps. Don't fear light overkill; you're unlikely to ever have all these lights on at the same time, and in their "off" setting, great lamps still function as jewelry for the room. A wide variety will let you create alluring pools of light in the evening and during parties, plus turn everything up when it's time to get some work done.

WALL ART AND ACCENTS

For spaces where you entertain guests, try a mix of large, mood-setting pieces and smaller conversation items. Too many things, and visitors can feel overwhelmed; too few, and the room can feel stark (unless, of course, you're going for calm minimalism intentionally).

Whenever possible, put light fixtures on dimmer switches so you can control the mood. When fully lit, an eight-arm chandelier will illuminate a space; when turned low for a party and supplemented with candlelight, it can create a festive or subtly romantic vibe.

RELAXING SPACES

BEDROOMS & DENS

A t the end of the day, everyone needs a private space to refresh, rest, and contemplate. Decorated with care, these places become your go-to spots to disconnect and decompress. But since they feel and function so differently than social spaces—less traffic, different storage needs, unique lighting requirements—furnishing and styling them requires a different set of guidelines. This chapter is dedicated to helping you create a bedroom, den, or master suite that calms and nurtures you—no matter your disposition or design aesthetic.

Who Thrives Here?

Sure, everyone sleeps, and everyone needs a calm place to unwind. But certain design dispositions fare particularly well in relaxing spaces and would do well to tackle them first. There are the Dream Weavers, who relish the mood shifts that come with moving from one distinct space to another, and for whom sensory elements can ease the transition to downtime. There are the Self-Expressionists, who revel in a room that reflects their own unique brand of mellow. Pragmatists may not be inclined to decorate a less "functional" room first, but they'll be rewarded once they do: after a hectic day, they'll be able to retreat to at least one room in the house that's totally done (and no doubt sleep better because of it).

That doesn't mean we leave Historians and Tinkerers out in the hallway. But they'll probably get less out of focusing their initial efforts on these spaces, because they're likely to put fewer purely decorative and sentimental pieces in the space and have less to arrange and rearrange.

Unfussy mix-and-match bedding makes a
guest room cozy and inviting for visitors. An
undersized vintage print adds personality above the
spooled wooden bed.

WHEN

FURNITURE
COMES FIRST

A piece of furniture with big
personality—say, a super-sleek
Japanese-style platform bed or an
ultraglamorous tufted Victorian
fainting couch—can override color
and lighting as the mood setter in
a relaxing space. If you have one of
these and intend to keep it, or if a
specific statement piece is on your
absolutely-gotta-have-it list, make
sure it's one of the first pieces to go
into your room mock-up.

Where to Begin

Wall color, textiles, and lighting will dictate the vibe of relaxing spaces
even more than social spaces, which tend to have multiple focal points and
functions. Here, it's all about the vibe, and that's created by the tactile and
the subtle—the way the curtains let light filter into the room (or don't), the
way a leather reading chair warms and conforms to your shape, or the way
bedside sconces cast a glow across your headboard.

If you have the opportunity, think through the materials and hues
you crave in the space as much as the dimensions, color, and shape of your
pieces: Are your pillows and curtains a casual, rumpled linen or a thick,
lustrous velvet? Are your dressers and nightstands formal and polished or
funky and distressed? Do you want the space to feel airy and clean (head
for the off-whites) or moody and enveloping (go for saturated tones)? Nail
these attributes down first, dropping digital paint swatches or images of
key materials into your room mock-up, then figure out which pieces fit the
bill for this aesthetic vision.

The same goes for lighting. Even if you don't identify the exact fixtures and lamps you'll put in a room, make some initial decisions about
where you want any ceiling or task lighting to go and what size it'll be,
so you can make other decisions, like which accent table to get, with the
future lighting in mind. The last thing you want is to buy a canopy bed that
crashes into the chandelier you had installed in the middle of the room or a
night table that's too small to hold the lamp you planned to have. The more
fleshed-out your room mock-up is before you begin making purchases, the
more likely everything will come together as planned.

Nightstands are totally optional.

Any number of pieces can work by the bed, not just nightstands. Here are six superb stand-ins.

- **A DRESSER.** Works for bedrooms big and small, as it can do double-duty as a bedside table and storage or help fill out a large space beside the bed.

- **A DESK.** If your bedroom doubles as an occasional office, try a simple parsons desk or skirted table by the bed.

- **AN ÉTAGÈRE.** An open-sided bookshelf offers space to display keepsakes, photos, and books. (Hello, Historians!)

- **A WALL-MOUNTED SHELF.** Hang one at nightstand height, and you'll get a spot for your must-haves without taking up any floor space.

- **A TRUNK.** Add storage to your bedroom by subbing a trunk for a night table. Just make sure the top is level enough for a lamp, or pair it with a wall-mounted sconce.

You don't need piles of plush cushions and coverlets for a bed to make a statement. A bold plum hue on the walls, a couple of easygoing toss pillows, and a single cheeky print above the headboard lend quirk and charm to this minimal master suite.

With matching lamps and bedside tables, a master bedroom can come off as über-polished and hotel-like, but an eclectic mix of patterned pillows keeps it feeling like home.

Room-Planning Guidelines

When selecting or rearranging furniture for a mellow, personal space, your activities are the most important consideration. Ask yourself, what is your brand of relaxing? Is it reading, watching TV, or listening to music in a really great chair? Then, as you select pieces, do all of the following before you buy:

- **Act it out.** What is the flow you imagine for this space? Are you kicking off your shoes, sitting down with a cup of tea, picking up a book, or falling right into bed? Walk through your space, going through the motions of an evening or afternoon break. Now, how does your furniture plan support that?

- **Focus on fit.** More so than any other room in the house, the furniture in bedrooms and dens should be comfortable for your physical proportions, whether you're four foot eleven or six foot six. Any seating you choose should be easy to get into and out of; your bed should suit your height and size. (So tall that your feet dangle? Try a California King.) This is not the place to put that not-so-comfy hand-me-down from your parents, if you can avoid it.

- **Layer the light.** Private, relaxing rooms call for lots of accent and task lighting, such as table lamps and wall-mounted sconces—not because you want to flood the room with lumens, but because points of light are far more soothing than a harsh overhead glow. Yes, it's important to have ample illumination when you're cleaning or running around packing for a trip, but for all other times, a balance of light and shadow is far more enticing.

- **Consider night *and* day.** Bedrooms don't often see a lot of foot traffic (or maybe yours does, in which case you're far more interesting than I am), but you still need to consider how humans move throughout the room, especially when lights are dim or off, and ensure there is ample space between chairs and tables, beds and walls. It's also important to avoid creating obstacles, like placing a table where you'll stub your toes on it nightly. Be sure to leave at least one and a half to two feet between pieces of furniture like chairs and low tables, and more for major walkways, to ensure there's enough space to pass through comfortably.

- **Note the difference between sitting and lounging.** What's comfortable for conversation in a busy living room may not be the same as what's comfortable for unwinding in a personal space at the end of the day. While you can employ many of the same principles for social spaces (see Chapter 6), like using chairs and rugs to create zones within a room, relaxation spaces call for a few tweaks. For instance, feel free to create a looser, lazier feel with deeper, lower-slung seating than you might use in a living room or formal parlor. And if you're deep in the relaxation zone, you're better off with a side table you can easily reach than a coffee table that forces you to shift your weight forward every time you want to put down your book or grab a sip of water.

- **Use artwork to cultivate the mood.** Aiming for a Zen retreat? A quirky sleeping space that makes you smile? Artwork around and above the bed can bring your theme to the forefront. Be selective: If your goal is for a romantic space, save the kids' coloring-book pages and school portraits for another room, and display pictures from that spa getaway instead. If you want a calm vibe, choose soft abstract art; to wake up energized, bold colors and graphics can work well.

- **Head off the clutter.** Whether it's a reading room teeming with piled books or a bedroom that tends to accumulate clothes, even the most carefully decorated room loses its appeal when it's covered in stuff. Whenever you're considering adding a new piece or swapping out an old one, ask yourself whether it's an opportunity to incorporate more storage. Think beds with hidden drawers, an étagère with baskets on the bottom two "floors," or a bench that opens up to store shoes and handbags.

Even the most CAREFULLY decorated room can lose its appeal when CLUTTER takes over.

◀◀ A grand headboard is the hero of this guest room. To keep things feeling light and airy, the homeowner opted for a tray table as the nightstand and a slim lamp with a clear glass shade.

➤➤ Dressed entirely in neutrals, this bedroom gets its personality from a delicious mix of textures: a heathered knit blanket, washed linen sheeting, wool-and-leather tassels, a wood-and-leather end table, and bunches of leafy eucalyptus.

One area that non-decorators always seem to struggle with is the end of the bed. It's typically an awkward space, but a clever combination of furniture can turn it into such a room-making statement. Here are a few of my favorite ways to dress those precious square feet.

THE LONG GAME

One long bench, with or without storage. Ideal for beds with a low (or nonexistent) footboard, as the combination of a large footboard and another piece of furniture can look heavy.

THE DYNAMIC DUO

Two square ottomans, with or without storage. Ideal for any bed. Serves the same function as the single long bench, but often looks better if there's a footboard, especially if you leave a small space between the ottomans.

THE CURL-UP SPOT

One small settee that's slightly less wide than the bed. Ideal for beds without a major footboard or canopy beds (for an extra-regal feel).

NOTHING AT ALL

Just as it sounds. Ideal for sleigh and panel beds with hefty footboards, small rooms, and minimalist aesthetics.

FIVE WAYS *TO STYLE A* BEDSIDE TABLE

Sure, a nightstand is mostly there to hold your lamp and your phone. But since it's the first thing you see every morning and the last thing you see at night, why shouldn't your bedside table get a little love and attention? From conventional nightstands styled with a bit of personal flair to broader interpretations of what belongs by the bed, these five looks are worth waking up to.

1

THE NONCONFORMIST

An open-sided bookshelf, also called an étagère, is an unexpected yet highly functional pick for pillow-side furniture. A lamp on top sheds light on evening reading, and open shelving puts all of your novels within reach. Decorative brass urchins add a little whimsy and help fill out the empty spaces.

BEST FOR:
Tinkerers, Self-Expressionists

2

THE NARRATIVE

Set beside a funky, sculptural lamp on a traditional wooden nightstand, an heirloom jewelry box offers a spot to place watches and rings, while an oversized black-and-white photo ensures every day ends with a good memory. A vintage sailcloth backdrop and a leafy plant potted in a mason jar help the arrangement feel anything but stodgy.

BEST FOR:
Historians, Dream Weavers

3

THE MULTITASKER

Where space is at a premium, a skirted table serves as both nightstand and writing desk, and a wall-mounted lamp is both a reading light and an additional desk light. A quartet of abstract watercolors centered over the desk helps to anchor the space, and a clear Lucite chair keeps the bed from feeling overwhelmed by furniture.

BEST FOR: Pragmatists

4

THE MINIMALIST

A petite round end table and a lamp with the simplest of profiles dress this edited bedside in style. A single framed photo and seasonal blooms add plenty of personality while leaving just enough room for a glass of water and a smartphone.

BEST FOR: Dream Weavers

5

THE MOOD LIFTER

Nestled by a modern copper-hued lamp, a vase of fragrant eucalyptus and a perfumed candle soothe the senses. A drawer in the nightstand lets other bedtime essentials remain out of sight and keeps the ambience simple and spa-like.

BEST FOR: Dream Weavers

TIP *Corral cords and wires using cable ties, or use a piece of masking tape to secure them to the back of your nightstand (with the plug on the nightstand surface), so your charging necessities don't end up in a constant tangle.*

Character Assessments

I always advise friends and family to avoid matching bedroom and sitting-room furniture sets like the plague, as they can instantly lend a bedroom an impersonal "showroom" feel. Worse, the pieces in a set are designed to relate to one another, not to create a well-balanced room, and they can quickly overwhelm a space as people try to shoehorn a wide dresser into a bedroom or an extra end table into a den.

Instead, I recommend choosing pieces that complement the things around them, be it the other furniture or the architecture of the space. Here are factors to consider when mixing and matching.

Visual weight. Think of the pieces in your space like a cast of characters on stage: they can't all be divas. If you have a commanding bed that is tall, has a thick mattress, or has a hefty wooden headboard and footboard, consider going lighter with the adjacent furniture and avoiding statement light fixtures. If you have a low-slung platform bed, the extra space between bed and ceiling may leave you room for an alluring oversize pendant light in the center of the room or two funky ceiling-hung lights beside the bed. Aim to balance the weight of items high and low, as well as across the space.

Materials. When it comes to bedroom furniture, materials matter. Polished wood can look warm and traditional; distressed and whitewashed wood often conveys a more rustic vibe. Matte painted colors can look cheerful and even country, while glossy, colorful lacquers feel preppy. Metal can go a number of ways, from industrial (think gears and pipes) to refined (gold leaf). Rattan has a breezy and sometimes retro vibe. Be thoughtful about how many looks and finishes you mix and match for a result that feels eclectic and purposeful, not hodgepodge.

◀◀ An inexpensive touch, fresh or faux flowers at the bedside add a sense of luxury to a room.

In the Details

No matter its size, look, or color scheme, a great relaxing space cultivates calm. Even if your decor choices in these rooms are lively and bold, selecting and placing pieces with the act of unwinding in mind will ensure you can actually power down in the space at the end of each day.

WINDOWS

Light control and privacy are equally, if not more important than, aesthetics. Whether you choose curtains on clips, rings, or grommets, or even automated shades, be sure that they open and close easily. And if you prefer to sleep in complete darkness, add a second rod and a blackout layer to block out the morning light.

LIGHTS

I've already made the case for having a lot of task and accent lighting. But making sure the styles you choose are as practical as they are pretty can be the difference between a look you like and a look you love to live in. Whether it's in a reading nook or by the bed, I love sconces that swing out and swivel, allowing you to position the light where you need it, and lamps with two or more light levels. If it's possible to change out your light switches for ones with dimmers, even better.

PILLOWS

I love pillows. Love, love, love them. But I've accepted that, for both my husband's sanity and my own, I can only have as many pillows as I'm willing to push out of the way when it's time to sit or lie down. It's also important to like the texture, not just the aesthetics, of any pillows you own. If furry things freak your partner out, don't put them on the bed. If beaded pillows scratch your neck, get rid of them. Comfort is key to setting a relaxing mood.

RUGS

Floor coverings are superb at defining spaces within a room, and they also act as noise dampeners—a must in rooms where you go to unwind. Oversize area rugs that cover most of the room are ideal if you don't already have carpeting, as nothing is more jarring than padding around in bare feet and landing unexpectedly on a patch of bare floor. Rugs can be pricey, however, so if you can't swing one that covers the floor on both sides of the bed, the foot of the bed, and/or a sitting area, consider combining several smaller rugs (such as a runner on each side of the bed and a medium-sized rug in the center of the room) for similar comfort and functionality.

SCENT

One could argue that how a room smells is not really part of its design. You could even say it's frivolous. Maybe so, but as a super-smeller (yes, I'm one of those), I can't stress enough what an impact fragrance can have on one's aesthetic experience of a space. The trick is to keep the scent subtle: I often purchase—but never light—scented candles, letting them faintly perfume the room over time. (Bonus: They last forever this way.) A linen spray, which you spritz onto sheets when you make the bed, is a lovely touch if you're so motivated, and some contain certain herbal fragrances, like lavender, that may actually help you sleep better. So give your room a signature scent. Why on earth not?

Skipping the matched
bed-in-a-bag set and dressing a
bed in your own mix of patterned
and solid textiles instantly gives
a room a homey, personal feel.
Here, linen sheets are topped with
a block-printed duvet, a lumbar
pillow, and an inexpensive cotton
throw, all in the same palette of
indigo, ivory, and taupe.

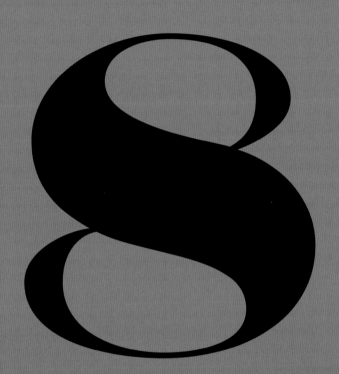

HARDWORKING
SPACES

KITCHENS, BATHROOMS & MUD ROOMS

They're either your favorite room of the house or your least favorite: the kitchen, bath, office, laundry, and mudroom. Because they seem hard to upgrade—"I can't afford to renovate!"—I find that people put off any kind of improvements at all to these spaces. But these are the rooms where life happens, so why not give them some love?

First off, I want to nip one idea in the bud, which is that you have to completely renovate in order to bring new life to your kitchen. Maybe you do need to renovate, but maybe it can wait. I've learned over the years that you can buy yourself more time to save and plan for those tear-out projects by making some decor moves that'll get your space into a "great for now" state. When my husband and I bought our first place, a condo, we knew that the one bathroom we had couldn't stay as it was: the Key lime-colored wainscoting, the rusting sconces, the comically small toilet. A renovation was off the table until we could save some money, but we were willing to dedicate $150 and a weekend to make it more in line with our tastes. I coated the whole room in white primer, which did double duty in saving us a step down the road. Running with the white theme, I put up white shelving, white-framed photos, and a white shower curtain. Pops of color came in the form of bath mats and a sprinkling of accents on the shelves. In the end, it became a space I didn't hate using several times a day—and that visitors even occasionally complimented.

But let's aim even higher and look at ways to make these spaces as eye-catching and functional as they can possibly be.

A hardworking space needs to FUNCTION well or you won't love it, no matter how many lovely things you fill it with.

Who Thrives Here?

Naturally, an über-functional yet also attractive room is cloud nine for Pragmatists, who crave order and efficiency. But Dream Weavers also often fantasize about ideal kitchens, especially if they are big home cooks. Historians and Self-Expressionists may find fewer opportunities to express their tastes in these rooms, but it's not entirely impossible, especially if your design leaves room for decorative accents and artwork on the walls. Tinkerers, likewise, may want to focus their early energies on rooms that are simpler to rework and reimagine.

Where to Begin

Outside of a true renovation, there are limits to what you can change in these spaces without serious construction, so your focus will likely be on optimizing the placement of accent furniture and storage pieces and nailing the decorative details.

Start by taking pictures of the space and dropping those images into your room mock-up. (If the current wall and cabinet colors are distracting or you're planning to change them, change the photo to black and white.) Drop in swatches of any new paint colors you're planning to add, so you can take them into consideration when choosing decorative touches.

- **Consider color.** I don't subscribe to the theory of choosing only hunger-inducing colors in the kitchen (orange and yellow) or spa colors in the bath (blue and green). Some of the best kitchens I've seen lean on deep, dramatic shades like navy, hunter green, or even glossy black. Be bold, even if only in your room mock-up. After all, if you can't experiment there, where can you?

◀◀ Thanks to brass-and-glass open shelving, light-colored walls, counters, and backsplash tiles, and a white island, a kitchen sporting dark blue lower cabinetry still feels airy and fresh.

➤➤ Glass surfaces reflect light in a dark-hued kitchen.

- **Incorporate your fixtures, appliances, and flooring materials.** A room is the sum of its parts, so don't leave out pictures of your current faucet fixtures, floor tiles, and the like. You'll want to see how everything relates.

- **Account for the adjacent spaces.** Is there a bold color or theme happening in the next room over? You'll want to be sure these spaces "talk" to one another and maybe even share some of the same colors so they feel like part of the same abode. This is especially important if you have one of today's ever-popular open floor plans, in which every space flows into the next.

➤➤ Noting that her party guests always tended to gather in the kitchen (Don't they always?), the owner of this home decided to incorporate a built-in spot for coffee and cocktails instead of a more formal dining table.

FIVE WAYS TO STYLE A
GALLERY WALL

For some reason, the act of combining several pieces of art on a single wall—a grouping often referred to as a gallery wall or salon wall—strikes fear in the heart of many would-be decorators. Maybe it's because the possibilities are endless: what to include, how to arrange the items, what frames to use, even how many pieces should be in the mix. These five approaches, however, are easy to execute, and one might be just right for your space.

THE UNIFIER

A wide variety of family photos—school portraits, vacation snaps, candids, wedding pictures—make up this informal-feeling arrangement. They key to pulling it together? All of the images are given the same black gallery frame and white double mat, no matter the size or subject.

 To avoid making a thousand "oops" nail holes in your walls, always map out your gallery arrangement before you hang a single piece. Either measure all your pieces and the wall and make a scale drawing of the whole design on paper first, or set up your gallery on the floor and take a picture of it so you can refer back to it as you go.

THE BIOGRAPHER

A race bib. A kid's drawing. A sheet of photo-booth pictures, a handful of sentimental photos, and more. They could add up to a hodgepodge, but thanks to a geometric layout (note the clear center line and two horizontal axes) and inexpensive white box frames, this snapshot of a family is crisp, clean, and full of personality.

THE CURATOR

Homemade brushstroke art mingles with photography, a mirror, and a vintage painting in this living room gallery. Despite the mix of mediums and the array of frame styles, keeping all of the pieces in a neutral palette makes for a cohesive-looking group.

THE BOLD STATEMENT

Large Rorschach-style inkblots make a graphic splash in this narrow but tall hallway gallery. Beveled gold frames mean the grid looks glam, not modernist or stark.

THE ANIMATED SERIES

One frame style unites this multicolored menagerie, made up of ten framed pages from photographer Catherine Ledner's book *Animal House*. Hung in two imperfect rows, this grouping fills a large wall and says "Don't take us too seriously." (Just look at it and try not to smile.)

Room-Planning Guidelines

Whether it's the room where you cook, bathe, or scramble together your belongings in the morning, every hardworking space needs to function well or you won't love it (no matter how many lovely things you fill it with). Here are the things to put first and foremost.

- **Ensure there's enough light.** Do you need to add lighting to augment the functionality of the space? There are lots of ways to do it, from strips of LEDs you can install under upper cabinets to stick-on lights you can place inside cabinets to sconces. Anywhere you do some fancy knife work, put on makeup, or grab a matching pair of shoes needs great light—otherwise you end up with unevenly cut veggies, uneven eyebrows, or mismatched footwear, and nobody likes that. While it's tempting to pick whatever fixture looks nice in your room mock-up, remember that if you replace a three-bulb fixture with a one-bulb mini-pendant, you're also going to lose some light. Pick purposefully.

- **Choose seating that's practical.** One of the most frequent mistakes I see is poorly proportioned and inaccessible seating, such as the too-high barstools that prevent people from eating comfortably at an island, the banquette seats in the eat-in kitchen that nobody can squeeze into, and the mudroom bench that's not large enough to sit on when you need to pull on a pair of boots. Measure as thoroughly as you can before you buy, even going as far as propping up a dining chair on books to test out different seat heights.

◀◀ With tall tub faucets arching over the sinks and Venetian mirrors that overlap the windows, a glamorous master bath breaks the rules in style. A countertop bust displaying a pretty watch and pendants proves that storage can be decorative, too.

⏩ As an alternative to closed cabinetry, open shelving offers storage while keeping the look casual and light. Here, shelves are styled with a mix of the functional (cookbooks, glassware, an espresso pot) and the decorative (a potted ponytail palm and a framed print).

- **Incorporate storage and ways to access it.** Do you need baskets, risers, and organizers inside your cabinets that help you make the most of every inch? Would having a step stool allow you to better utilize high cabinets and shelves? Consider the storage capabilities of everything you bring in, from rolling kitchen carts to freestanding cabinets and pot racks. More than any other areas of your home, working rooms need to accommodate your belongings and then some, which will prevent your excess stuff from getting in the way of your day-to-day functioning.

- **Make your most-used items accessible.** Whether it's the toaster you use every day, the curling iron you reach for every morning, or the sports gear your kids grab every afternoon at two o'clock, frequently used items need a front-and-center home in the space. That doesn't mean they have to be visible in an open basket, but they should be where you need them when you need them. Resist the urge to design your room around the showpiece stand mixer if you're not a baker, or an umbrella holder if you live in the desert, and give priority to the stuff you use more.

*Be sure
your spaces
"TALK"
to one another so
they feel like
part of the same
ABODE.*

Character Assessments

As you select and filter the pieces that'll live in the space, think about what you want the room to feel like. Is it a work space, or do you prefer that functionality remains hidden? Would you rather create a sense of visual drama, or do you like tidy utility? Below are some questions to ask yourself as you layer items into (or remove them from) your space.

- **Should you put things away or keep them out in the open?** There are two approaches to being organized. One is to have a closed cabinet or cubby where everything can be invisibly stashed; the other is to have everything you need within easy reach.

- **Do you want people to perch, or do you prefer them to hang?** In other words, how comfortable and/or private do you want these spaces to be? This is not just a question for kitchens; I've seen a surprising number of bathrooms and dressing rooms with comfy seating in them as a place for a partner to sit and chitchat while you soak and get dressed. The more plush and loungy the furniture you place in these rooms, the more likely people will camp out in them.

- **Is this a home base or a showplace?** Are you a frequent entertainer, or is this a space that only family will generally see? Knowing this might steer you toward more or less formal materials.

◀◀ Featuring a brass swan faucet and an ornate bejeweled mirror, a phone booth–sized powder room is big on glamour. The wallpaper is a now-iconic design by Ellie Cashman.

In the Details

The title of this section is a bit misleading, because unless you're renovating your kitchen or installing mudroom or bathroom cabinets, every
decision you'll be making is detail-oriented. But giving extra attention to
things that could be grab-'em-without-thinking purchases like doormats
and a new faucet—and making those decisions with as much care as you
would use when choosing a new sofa or dining table—will ensure that your
high-functioning spaces are as beautiful as they are useful.

Bistro-style wooden chairs with a
rustic oak finish feel homey and
help to balance this kitchen's showier
elements, like polished-brass baker's
racks and navy cabinetry in a high-
gloss finish.

A simple tray corrals cocktail fixings and keeps bottles looking tidy when left out on the countertop. When happy hour arrives, the whole tray can be carried to the living room or dining table.

Coveting a graphic marble floor tile but cognizant of her budget, this bathroom's owner opted to create "bath mats" of patterned mosaic tile in front of the dual sinks instead of installing it across the entire floor.

In the same bathroom, faceted-glass drawer pulls hang like jeweled pendants from the clean white double vanity, dressing up the space.

Square tiles with matte gold corners create a modern geometric diamond pattern on a kitchen backsplash. The gold tone is echoed by the brushed-brass drawer hardware, which finishes the look.

◀◀ To keep open kitchen shelving looking clean, not cluttered, use it to store and display a matched (or at least monochrome) set of glassware or dinnerware.

RUGS

Scatter rugs, runners, and mats add a layer of pretty softness to these spaces, which can easily go "cold" or "hard" due to the angles of the cabinetry and the cool metal of appliances. Indoor/outdoor rugs are great choices, as they can be taken outside and hosed off if they get a little grungy; vintage or distressed rugs, especially wool ones, are designed to take a beating and withstand repeated cleanings. For maximum dirt camouflage, choose a rug with a darker color or a busier pattern that will hide stains. To state the obvious, it's best to avoid pale rugs in these hardworking spaces.

As for size, look for runners and mat-size rugs that measure about two-thirds to three-quarters of the width of the floor space they're covering, leaving a healthy border between the edge of the rug and any walls or cabinets. You should still be able to swipe a broom around the rug for quick cleanups.

OPEN SHELVES AND COUNTERTOP STORAGE

In recent years, there's been a move toward including more open shelves in kitchens, baths, laundry rooms, and mudrooms, utilizing these surfaces to display necessities. Countertops, too, are being shown as places to communicate your personal style. But to ensure they work for real life requires a certain amount of curation. On counters, aim to keep at least the front two-thirds clear, otherwise all of that decorative-yet-practical stuff will start encroaching upon your work space. On open shelves, leave out only items you grab and use weekly, lest items start to accumulate dust, and try to make sure you're not reaching for the same three glasses every time. If your open-shelf arrangement includes decor, make sure the purely ornamental pieces don't obstruct your access to the things you need to handle daily.

◀◀ High-quality high-gloss paint on cabinetry is actually more resistant to nicks and dings than your typical eggshell or matte finish, making it a good choice for heavily trafficked kitchens.

HARDWARE AND LIGHTING

Just say no to builder-grade details! The hardware, plumbing, and light fixtures that come with many new and recently renovated homes is often bland and lower-quality. If you're able to make some swaps, use your room mock-up as a place to try out different combinations of metal finishes when you replace what you have. Matching is easiest, but it can make a space feel slightly one-note (imagine a kitchen with brushed-stainless faucets, pendant lights, appliances, and cabinet hardware), so I encourage people to get a little brave and try adding at least one other material into the mix. If you do combine multiple finishes, strive for some degree of repetition (such as using oiled bronze on both the cabinets and the pendant lights, but going stainless on the faucets to match the appliances) to tie it all together.

SEATING

When it comes to choosing kitchen seating, mudroom benches, and even accent seating for a large master bath, it's important to choose the right breed of seat for your goals. In the kitchen, a common mistake is to select too-tall or too-small seats for dining at the island, leaving guests with their chins just above their plates or their legs pressed against the underside of the counter. For counter-height dining, choose counter-height stools (twenty-four inches to twenty-six inches tall), while bar-height stools (twenty-eight inches to thirty inches tall) should be used if the dining surface is true bar height (raised above the work surface). Then there's the issue of backless versus backed stools. My rule of thumb? If most meals are served at the island, think seriously about bringing in backed stools for added comfort. Otherwise, backless stools are great space savers, as they can be tucked under the counter when not in use. In mudrooms, choose benches and chairs that are low enough for you to easily bend down and tie a shoe.

Finally, what material suits the seating in hardworking spaces best? No matter how tidy the homeowner, bathrooms, kitchens, and mudrooms are prone to splashes, smudges, and spills. Consider wood and metal, which are easy to wipe clean. If you prefer cushioned seating, choose printed fabrics that show fewer spots or stools with slipcovers that can be removed and washed. For a best-of-both-worlds situation, seats upholstered in leather, faux leather, or an indoor/outdoor fabric like Sunbrella are highly practical picks.

⏩ Parisian brasserie decor inspired the design of this city kitchen, from the bentwood Thonet counter stools to the industrial pendants, honed marble counters, and cast-iron brackets supporting the wall shelves and island.

◀◀ Removable wallpaper sporting leafy birch trees, used on one accent wall, brings life to a kids' bathroom.

◀◀ An oversize European landscape and a vignette of coordinating decor prove every space—even the washroom—can benefit from a bit of whimsy.

COLOR

Make sure any color you incorporate doesn't create a big imbalance in the space. If your only splash of brightness is a set of red counter stools far on one side of the kitchen, the room might end up feeling lopsided. Create balance by adding a bit more color on the opposite side, either by dressing opposing shelves with colorful pottery or plants or choosing towels and other accessories that add oomph elsewhere.

That doesn't mean you can't bring in one statement splash of color in a room, however, like a bold light fixture hanging in the center or a giant piece of art in the foyer. As long as it's near the middle of the space and doesn't tip the visual balance of the room toward one wall or the other, a single bold color move can be a very, very good thing indeed.

▶▶ Caged in chicken wire, a glass globe pendant illuminates a sink area and adds vintage charm.

ART AND OBJECTS

Even the most purpose-built rooms deserve a decorative flourish. Framed prints, sculptural pottery, and functional decor such as clocks all add life to a working space, taking it from catalog-chic to charmingly real. Layer pictures of these details into your room mock-up to help you decide which ones complement the mood you've created with lights, color, and fixtures.

UNEXPECTED TOUCHES

Try a basket instead of a standard trash can in the powder room. And why not a crystal chandelier over the island or an enormous palm tree by the kitchen door? The unconventional choices you make in your bathroom, kitchen, and laundry room—often some of the most cookie-cutter corners of a home—can really have an impact on how "you" your home feels.

◀◀ Swirling blue wallpaper isn't the only statement piece in this powder room. A moody portrait, purchased from a vintage shop and hung above the toilet tank, is an unexpected addition.

🌷 Just off a Paris-inspired kitchen, a bathroom door sports a detail seen in many a French brasserie: a WC ("water closet") sign.

IN-BETWEEN
SPACES

ENTRIES, HALLWAYS, BREEZEWAYS & STAIRS

I t's so easy to focus on just the rooms in which we "live"—the bedrooms, family rooms, kitchens, and baths. But there's more to a home than that. When considered instead of overlooked, in-between spaces like foyers, hallways, entries, landings, and stairwells have the power to make a residence feel finished and full. Whether public or private, highly trafficked or occasionally passed through, the in-between spaces are ones of both transition and welcome. Why not give them their due?

Who Thrives Here?

As spaces that bridge other spaces have a less-than-distinct identity, they're an ideal playground for Tinkerers, who can recast them as the surrounding spaces and their daily needs evolve. And since they're also well suited to gallerylike displays of art and personal mementos, they're perfect places for Historians to work their magic. Front-of-the-house transition spaces like foyers, if they make a big statement, can cause both Dream Weavers and Self-Expressionists to swoon. And if redoing the in-between spaces solves an organization issue or improves flow through the house, Pragmatists will be pleased as punch, too. In short, these parts of the house have the potential to delight everyone when decorated well.

*An
IN-BETWEEN
space should make
you SMILE,
or at least make
you want to know
what's in the space
BEYOND.*

◄◄ By pushing a desk up
against a window in a living room,
this homeowner carved out
space for a home office. An eclectic mix
of modern and timeworn
decor surrounding the desk keeps
the workspace from feeling
like an afterthought.

Where to Begin

Though they may not have four walls (or even any windows), in-between spaces like hallways and entries have the potential for big visual impact. And because they're open to other spaces, they have the power to unify disparate rooms of the home. For that reason, I like to choose a wall color first, so you can be sure that the nook in question coordinates with all of the other spaces it touches. (If you wait to choose paint until the end, it can be quite the challenge to find the one hue that ties everything together.) When making a room mock-up of a hall or entry, it's helpful to place swatches of the adjacent spaces' key colors off to the side, so you can keep them in mind when selecting your wall color as well as the decorative details.

Next I like to select the case goods (that is, hard furniture like tables, chests, and cabinets) that the area needs, since these spaces can be awkwardly sized, and since there tend to be space constraints to consider. You don't want to limit your furniture options because of the rug you chose or the color of the frames you put on the wall. Hallways can be hard enough to furnish without all those extra factors.

In the breezeway of a Spanish-style home, decorative versions of essential features, like a copper-flower rain chain in lieu of a gutter downspout, make the "between" spaces as charming as can be.

A small accent chair transforms this empty corner of a room into a reading space; hanging a framed photo beside the chair makes the seat's placement feel purposeful. Plants above and on the adjacent table add vibrant life and texture.

Room-Planning Guidelines

Because they're often non-enclosed, non-square areas with corners and doorways galore, in-between spaces require thinking differently about your furnishings and decorations. Here are some of the strategies I've found helpful over the years.

- **Think in visual moments.** What do you see from this landing, that doorway, or when you're peeking up the stairs? Whatever it is, it should make you smile, or at least make you want to know what's in the space beyond. Hints of decor help communicate that the space continues and that you're not looking into a storage space. As you make your decor plan, think of that view as a scene or moment, and try to create a mock-up that reflects your ideal visual snapshot.

- **Define a function.** Where it makes sense, carve out a "room" within the space. Whether it's a workstation, a console you'll utilize as you go through your daily routine, or an overflow pantry, make sure it truly functions as such. In other words, don't just throw any desk in the hall and think you'll be happy to pay bills there once a month, and don't put an armoire in the hall and call it a linen closet. Make sure the space is dressed and accessorized for what it's intended to be, incorporating storage and small touches that'll make it work for its newly defined purpose.

- **Lead with rugs and runners.** Runners and rugs help to "cozy up" a space, make hallways seem larger, and signal to the brain that it is, in fact, part of the home and not just an alley between rooms. A good rule of thumb for hallways is that runners should be wide enough to leave just four to six inches of floor exposed on either side. Whether the rug spans the entire length of a hall or is just an accent in the center portion, choose a size that lets a person entering the hallway land either completely on or completely off of it (not one foot on and one foot off).

- **Ensure adequate light.** Hallways, entries, and foyers aren't always the first places that you'd think to bring in a lamp. But if you're lacking in windows or relying solely on ceiling fixtures to illuminate the space, additional lighting can greatly increase the ambience and bring life to an overlooked area. Try a pair of tall table lamps on a console or converting a recessed light into a hanging pendant, which will bring the light source closer to eye level.

- **Showcase a collection.** Console tables and floating shelves provide ideal surfaces for displaying ephemera in an entry or hallway or on a landing. You don't need to be a dedicated collector in the traditional sense to craft an intriguing display; a collection can be any visually interesting thing that you have in multiples, such as an array of old cameras, a variety of straw hats, or a mix of potted houseplants. Whatever the items, grouping and treating them as sculpture will lend them an artful presence.

- **Don't forget doors.** Some of the most smile-inducing touches I've seen in homes are around the doors: pretty tassels hung from the knobs, a vintage iron or a weighted sailor's knot used as a doorstop, a decorative hook placed between a door's inset panels. Even simply painting the hall side of the doors in a surprising hue (say glossy navy or jet black, if it works with the whole-house scheme) can bring incredible life to a space.

◀◀ Matching decor, like the pair of identical lamps and the coordinated prints above this console, tends to have a formalizing effect on a space. If you prefer to set a more relaxed tone, mix things up.

FIVE WAYS
TO STYLE A
BOOKSHELF

An expanse of shelving can be either totally inspiring or completely paralyzing to decorate. Since most of us have the ingredients for a great display—books, magazines, picture frames, and the odd vase or bowl—already on hand, it's tempting to try and throw everything together in one go. At the same time, shelves are such a prominent display of your style, it's easy to get hit with decorating stage fright. Fortunately, there's no "right" setup—no perfect ratio of books to art to goofy souvenirs. Consider these five takes on open shelving, and which might suit your style (and your stuff) best.

1
THE CLASSIC

Vintage metal vessels, traditional porcelain pieces, and brass candlesticks mingle with contemporary decorative objects against a crisp, white backdrop. Leafy plants, coffee-table books, and hardcover reads help fill in the gaps.

BEST FOR:
Dream Weavers, Historians

2
THE ECLECTIC ACADEMIC

A mix of tightly stacked books and found objects, this free-form setup works in bookshelves of all shapes and sizes. It elevates even simple paperbacks and begs visitors to peruse the spines.

BEST FOR:
Self-Expressionists,
Historians, Pragmatists

3
THE MONOCHROME

Keep it simple with a coordinated display of pieces in a unified palette. What prevents this combination from looking flat and staged? A smart mix of materials (metal, glass, bone inlay, paper) that bring texture and a range of neutrals (mahogany, ecru) that balance the bold blacks and whites.

BEST FOR:
Dream Weavers

4
THE BOTANIST

Sculptural succulents and leafy trailing plants make for an arrangement that brims with life and changes with each day. Framed family photos, typographic art, and petite decor pieces fill the shelves with layers of personality.

BEST FOR:
Self-Expressionists, Tinkerers

5
THE 3-D ARTIST

By layering short book stacks, sculptural decor, storage pieces, and accents from top to bottom and back to front, this asymmetric display makes the most of a deep alcove. Narrow but tall decor and a perky cactus help break the boundaries between shelves.

BEST FOR:
Self-Expressionists,
Historians, Tinkerers

TIP ▶▶ *Don't own many books? Make barren shelves look fuller by laying the tomes you have in horizontal stacks and topping them with candles, paperweights, or other objects. As you accumulate books, you can eventually turn them vertically.*

Character Assessments

As you fill out your plan with paint, furniture, and decor, think about both the shape and spirit of each element. Here are a few points to consider.

Choose pieces with personality. Because hallways, entries, and landings are so exposed, and because they can lack a sense of purpose, I love to see items with outsize personalities showcased here. Charm, then, becomes the purpose of the space. That item could be an antique armchair with elaborate lines, a modernist table crafted from a unique material, or a runner in a dramatic geometric print. Maybe it's an art piece with a sense of cheeky humor or photos that transport you to a favorite destination. Have fun! Hallways and landings are great places to put your personality on display without seeming self-absorbed (compare it to putting an oversize family portrait above the living room fireplace).

Define a pace. Do you want people to pause in your hallways or pass through quickly en route to other "destination" spaces of the home? The artwork you choose can help drive the experience. Photos invite visitors to stop and examine, while abstract artwork is easier to breeze by.

Bridge your styles. If the various rooms of your home are worlds apart in style, you can utilize the in-between space as a buffer to tie your disparate looks together. In a hallway between a cottage-style living room and a modern bedroom, for example, you might echo the color palette of the living room but furnish the space with a sleeker contemporary table and wall art that's more in line with the bedroom's aesthetic. A stairwell leading from a very traditional floor to a modern addition might call for vintage prints in crisp gallery-style frames. Aim to ease the transition with creative combinations.

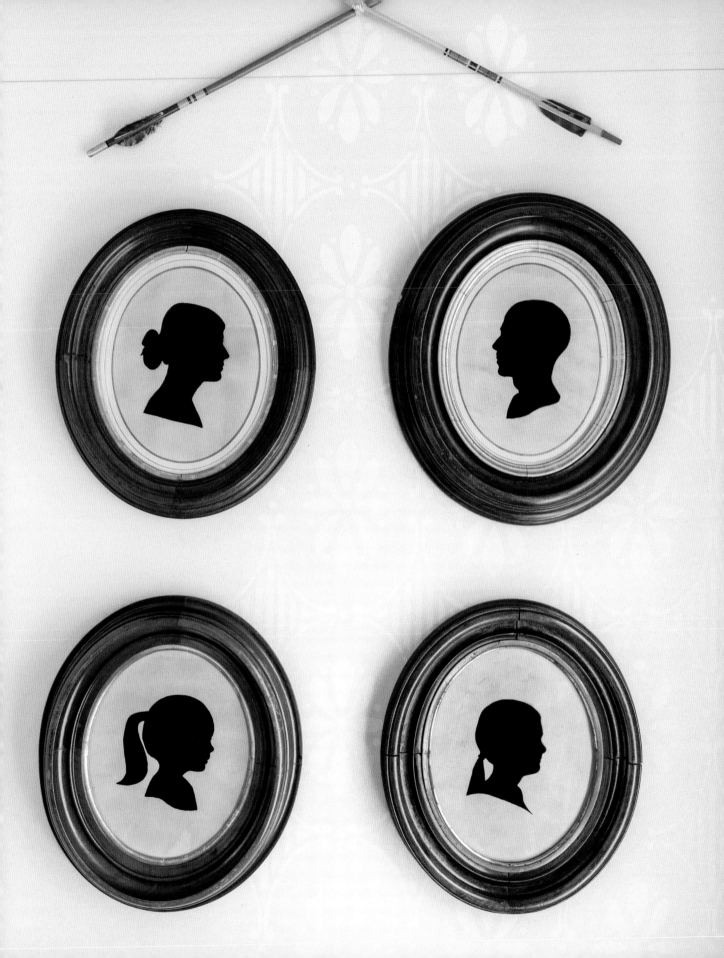

If the various rooms of your home are WORLDS apart in style, utilize the in-between space as a BUFFER to tie your disparate looks TOGETHER.

◄◄ In addition to filling out an awkward space between a dining area and living room, a midcentury-style chair and companion plant stand add a pop of verdant color.

In the Details

In-between spaces are all about the details—the little touches and design decisions that add comfort, charm, and delight. Taking extra care when choosing the following elements for your hallways, stairways, entries, and more can make all the difference between spaces that feel like dressed-up passageways and places that truly complete your home's story.

SEATING

Make sure the seats you choose are suited to the function you're hoping to create. If you're looking to carve out an area for reading or work, a wider, deeper chair is the way to go, provided there's enough room for one. If the seats are just meant for a quick sit as you're waiting to head out the door, consider an armless chair or repurposing extra dining chairs not in use outside of the holidays.

MIRRORS

Mirrors are a tremendous addition to halls, foyers, and entries, as they reflect light and tend to make the spaces feel larger. If they're purely decorative, choose the location based on where you would hang a piece of art: as a focal point at the end of the hallway, perhaps, or centered between two doorways. But if the mirror is intended for checking your lipstick or outfit on your way out the door, make sure it's large enough—and hung at the right height—to give yourself a once-over as you depart.

An antique Oriental rug adds subdued pattern and color to a traditional townhouse's small entryway.

A sofa in a kitchen? Yes, it can work. This space, located by a back entrance and across from the kitchen island, lacked purpose until its occupants turned it into the perfect place to curl up with coffee and a newspaper.

PENDANT LIGHTS

It can be challenging to gauge the right height for any hanging fixtures, as the lights don't typically hang over an "anchor" piece such as a dining table, bed, or kitchen island that you'd use as a reference point. Aim instead for a comfortable walk-under height—typically, this means the bottom of the fixture should hang about eight feet above the floor. Be sure to account for any rooms that open into the entry or hall to avoid hitting the fixture with a swinging door.

FUNCTIONAL DECOR

Hooks, hall trees, and umbrella stands are logical additions to in-between spaces that sit near an entrance or exit of your home. But try to avoid choosing one simply based on the function of the piece; these items can have character, too, and their look can impact the aesthetic of the entire space. Shop for them just as you would shop for wall art or furniture, looking for pieces that marry both the purpose you seek and the look and feel you want for the room. Flea markets and antiques fairs can be great resources for finding functional pieces with character, but you can also think outside the box. Why not mount cabinet knobs or doorknobs as a funky place for your coats or use a tall basket to stow umbrellas? (Just place a dish at the bottom to catch drips.) How about a floating wall shelf as a stand-in for a hall console in a narrow space? Go for it. Don't be afraid to improvise.

EQUAL
but different
1 tsp = 1/6 fl oz = 1/3 Tbsp
1 Tbsp = 1/2 fl oz = 3 tsp
1/8 cup = 1 fl oz = 2 Tbsp
1/4 cup = 2 fl oz = 4 Tbsp
1/2 cup = 4 fl oz = 8 Tbsp
1 cup = 8 fl oz = 1/2 pint
1 pint = 16 fl oz = 2 cups
1 quart = 32 fl oz = 2 pints
1 gallon = 128 fl oz = 4 quarts

RUGS

In-between spaces tend to be what rug manufacturers call "high-traffic zones." Walking is the main activity here, and even if you're a shoe-free household, the rugs in these spaces tend to take a beating. Consequently, they require a level of stain resistance and durability far beyond what you'd need in a bedroom or dining room, where people mostly just sit around. Shag rugs? Not here. The best bets are generally low-pile versions or even flatweaves in dirt-concealing colors or patterns. Wool is great if you can afford it, but synthetics are also a fine option. Cotton rugs are more prone to soiling, but they can also be thrown in the wash. Either way, read online reviews and avoid styles known to shed profusely, which high traffic will exacerbate. (Some shedding is normal, but it shouldn't continue for months or years on end.)

The best options for in-between spaces, however, may be vintage or faux-distressed rugs, which won't look worse with wear, as well as indoor/outdoor rugs, which can be hosed off when they get dirty. Whatever you choose, a rug pad is a must, not because you need the extra cushioning, but because it will help your rug stay put when there's a lot of back-and-forth traffic.

PLANTS

I love the idea of bringing potted plants and indoor trees into an in-between space, both for the color and natural ambience they add. Whether you pick leafy palms or feathery ferns, be sure to choose a variety of species that will thrive with the light levels in your space and the maintenance you're willing to provide, from watering to fertilizer. My favorite low-maintenance houseplants for low- to medium-light conditions include ferns, philodendrons, pothos, peace lilies, succulents, and ponytail palms. If your plant will live by a window, consider fig varieties, ficuses, spider plants, rubber plants, and aloes.

◄◄ Furnished with an outdoor love seat dressed with weather-resistant pillows, a Spanish-style home's petite veranda becomes a welcoming spot to relax.

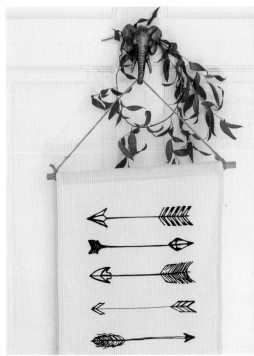

▶▶ Even the back of a door is an opportunity to show some personality. Here, a simple banner and a wreath of preserved greenery find a home on a charming brass elephant hook.

10

KIDS' SPACES

BEDROOMS & PLAYROOMS

Furnishing and decorating for our home's smallest residents presents many great style opportunities but also many challenges. In nurseries, kids' bedrooms, and playrooms, there's a need to balance fun with function, preciousness with practicality, and the desire to spoil ("They're only young once!") with the need to save (Hello, college tuition!).

Done well, though, a kid's space works just as well as any other. It's comfortable, the furniture supports the key activities of sleep, play, and storage, and the decorative touches bring it to life. And I mean *real* life: This chapter is not a guide to creating grand, catalog-perfect bedrooms full of monogrammed chairs and decorative toys they're not allowed to touch. It's about creating happy rest-and-recreation spots for babies, toddlers, and big kids. The keys are planning for the stuff you need—or want—to buy, combining it smartly with the stuff you already have, and arranging everything so it makes you and your little ones smile.

Who Thrives Here?

Unlike other rooms in the home, kids' bedrooms and playrooms serve many masters—usually some a few decades older than the others. This can bring confusion to the decorating process from the get-go, as the person deciding what stays and goes is typically not the one who'll end up calling the space his or her own.

Your disposition as parent or decorator can also differ greatly from your kids', posing another challenge. If you're a Pragmatist, for example, you may gravitate toward order-creating filing systems for homework, art, and toys, or you might lean toward utilitarian, durable furnishings that will withstand years of abuse (and stick around through the college years). Your kid, meanwhile, could be a Self-Expressionist who loves being surrounded by posters and an art collection, or a Tinkerer who'll ask to redecorate in a year.

The bottom line is, putting together a kids' space will probably push you outside your own natural comfort zone, and that might mean it takes a little more time to create a plan you love. But that's a good thing. Here's why:

- There are multiple people with varying dispositions involved, and each has a right to love the room.

- Kids' spaces beg for constant change, even when everyone's happy with the way they look. (For example, your teenager will need more clothes storage than a four-year-old, and those toy chests will likely be edged out in favor of bookshelves and beanbags.)

- Kids' furniture is generally inexpensive (or it can be if you're willing to get creative), making decor choices less risky.

◄◄ A lofted bed leaves room underneath for a pile of pillows. A wide range of patterns, from thick cabana stripes to an abstract leaf print, makes for a playful, informal space.

➨ A fill-your-own lamp packed with toy dinosaurs adds fun to a little boy's bedside. Beneath, a glass-and-brass end table stands in for a traditional nightstand.

Where to Begin

Oddly enough, I like to start most kids'-room plans with a rug. Children's bedrooms and playrooms tend to have more open floor space than other rooms (to accommodate for tumbling and fort building, of course), and that puts your rug choice in the spotlight. Whether it's patterned, solid, or even shag, your floor covering will provide a stylistic anchor for these ever-evolving spaces through the teen years, and large ones can be costly, so there's a good case for selecting and dropping them into your room mock-up first. (The exception is if you already have a large, style-specific statement piece, like a painted dresser or a big piece of art, that you're planning to use in the space. In that case, that item will be the key influencer for your rug, decor, and furniture choices.)

But what about wall color? Many soon-to-be parents choose a nursery hue almost as soon as they know their baby's sex, thinking they have to select a paint color before any other part of their baby girl's or boy's space. This may surprise you, but I don't think of paint as a choose-it-first component of the room. Kids are brutal on walls, so you're likely to need to repaint the space every few years anyway, and it's a fun choice to involve a kid in. So pull a paint color from one of the hues in the rug, decor pieces, or bedding (see "Design Revelation #10, page 203"), and move along.

DESIGN
REVELATION
№ 9

Nurseries are for parents.

If the room you're working on is for a newborn baby, your design choices aren't really for the baby—they're for you. After all, who's to say that your kid will like robots, baby elephants, or whatever else ends up in your design scheme? Truth be told, all babies want is a quiet, warm place to be rocked, a safe crib to sleep in, and a comfy spot to have their diaper changed (even if that's the floor). By all means, decorate away—I've done it for my kids twice, and the point of this chapter is to help you do it better. It's a lovely way to show yourself and others that you're ready for this new addition to your home and family. But if preparing a nursery is a stressor rather than a pleasure, spare yourself the pregnant scramble. You'll have plenty of chances to reimagine the space as your child grows and starts to have preferences of his or her own.

⇒ Shades of ivory, gray, and black make for a perfectly gender-neutral nursery. A mismatched set of furniture—black crib, white armoire—feels collected rather than bought all at once.

As for selecting beds and seating, be aware that kids' needs for these pieces will change constantly as they grow—even more reason not to design a room around a crib or rocking chair. But while they're not forever pieces, they are big and important, and your choices can impact the amount of space you have available for other things like play tables and bookshelves. Make sure they're included in the mocking-up and planning process.

Finally, make an effort to involve your kid, too. You can mimic the same process described in Chapter 2 ("Defining Your Aesthetic"): Have your child point out images from magazines or the Internet and prod them to explain what they like about each space. Do they repeatedly select spaces with bold graphics and strong themes? You'll do well to pick furnishings and décor that make a statement. Are they partial to soft palettes and spaces that seem plucked from a fairytale castle? Head toward the pastels and neutrals. You might also notice that your child prefers rooms that look more like playrooms or classrooms—full of activities and stimulating details—or that they zero in on calm, enveloping hideaways, and make your selections with this in mind. At the same time, remember that kids are impulsive and their tastes change, so think twice about commissioning any pricey built-ins or whole-room murals because your child liked it in a picture they saw on the web.

Room-Planning Guidelines

Whether it's a bedroom or a dedicated playroom, a room in which kids spend any length of time needs to consider delight and "Does it work?" in equal measure. In this case, work means that kids can safely and happily access what they want to, when they want to, and aesthetics don't get in the way of activity. These guidelines can help.

- **Designate zones for sleep, dressing, play, and homework.** Help kids help themselves. If a child has to reach past toys to bring school books to his or her desk or walk across the room to get from the hamper to the dresser, it can take him or her longer to get through the daily routine. As much as you can, place items that are typically used together near one another, such as a shelf for favorite bedtime books near the bed.

- **Allow for empty fields.** In a dining room or adult bedroom, it might seem strange to have a wide stretch of floor that's totally free of furniture. But in a kid's room? That empty space is a dance floor one day, a stage or a pillow fort the next. Resist the urge to fill it up.

- **Incorporate storage.** Then incorporate more. You'll thank yourself for including lots of storage in any kid's space, both dedicated (like bookshelves and freestanding cubby units) and hidden (such as a storage ottoman or a dresser tucked under a lofted bed). No matter how much storage you have, you'll always wish you had more.

- **Keep lighting simple.** While living rooms and other adult spaces call for a wide variety of mood-setting illumination options, from recessed lights overhead to floor lamps, task lamps, and sconces, kids don't care to flip multiple switches and knobs throughout the day. Aim to have one primary light source overhead that's strong enough to flood the whole room, then layer in just a few accent lights, such as a desk lamp for homework and a reading lamp for bedtime stories. And don't forget the night-light!

- **Skip decor for decor's sake.** With the exception of wall art, I'm not a fan of decorative objects that kids aren't allowed to touch—especially not when retailers today have adorable bookends, night-lights in modern forms, and even white-noise machines in charming animal shapes. Lean on these decorative-yet-functional (and more important, child-safe) must-haves to add that last layer of interest, and leave the porcelain figurines at the flea market.

FIVE WAYS TO STYLE A
CONSOLE

Whether it's a table in a hall or entryway, a dining room sideboard, or a long surface behind a sofa, consoles often play a supporting role to some other piece of furniture or simply exist to help fill in space. With thoughtful styling, though, they can be a dramatic and highly personal feature of a home. Here are five different takes, each with a look and function all their own.

1
THE PREP STATION

A mirror to check your lipstick. A bowl or tray to catch your keys. And a little decorative something—plant, sculpture, picture frame—that seems to say "See you soon," or "Welcome home." That's all it takes to create an entryway that'll greet you warmly every day of the week.

BEST FOR:
Pragmatists

2
THE STAGE

One statement-making piece is the star of this show. Surrounded by a supporting cast, including gleaming faux-horn accents and a pair of alabaster lamps on each end of the table, an antique, gold-leafed Buddha statue earns reverence.

BEST FOR:
Dream Weavers, Historians

3
THE SCENE-SETTER

Though small, a vintage marble-topped telephone table hints at the quirky yet classic look of the space beyond. A single framed print and bud vase add charm without fuss, and a piece of clear glass decor adds interest without making the petite surface feel overcrowded.

BEST FOR:
Self-Expressionists, Tinkerers

4
THE VIGNETTE

A chest of drawers in a hallway or alcove provides the perfect opportunity to showcase some personal style. A bright abstract print brings in a pop of color, a stack of neutral books gives it lived-in appeal, and an oversized lamp creates a little pool of light to take it all in.

BEST FOR:
Dream Weavers

5
THE CABINET OF CURIOSITIES

A vintage sideboard serves as a display surface for an array of quirky wares, as well as storage for other items that can be rotated in as the mood strikes. The current exhibit: an heirloom jewelry tin, a brass candle lantern, and a diminutive teapot. A vintage print, leaned instead of permanently hung, can be easily swapped out to create a different vibe.

BEST FOR:
Historians, Self-Expressionists, Tinkerers

TIP ➡
Consoles and sideboards go by many aliases. If you're looking for a long, narrow piece to display decor, try searching for sofa table, narrow desk, credenza, media console, hall table, *or* buffet table. *Whatever the retailer or furniture maker calls it, if you like the look of the piece and the dimensions suit your space, you can use it for whatever you please.*

Character Assessments

Furnishing and decorating a livable, lovable kid's space will prove easier—and often more fun—if you skip the matching suite of products and create your own mix. You'll have an easier time adding and removing pieces as the kid's needs evolve, and the result is a more collected, charismatic look. Here are a few pointers.

- **Think beyond "kid" furniture.** You don't need to shop out of a youth-furniture catalog to dress a kid's room well; vintage and contemporary adult furniture can be just as well suited to a child's room and is often of a higher quality. Instead of a nursery glider, try an antique rocking chair or an upholstered armchair-and-ottoman combo. And consider what items you might bring in from elsewhere in your home, such as a dresser that could be painted and topped with a pad to become a changing table, or an unused end table that could work by the reading or nursing chair.

- **Choose pieces with the potential to grow or move.** Just as you might repurpose your own former armchair for a kid's space, think of where each new item you bring in might work down the road. Will that side table be large enough to be a nightstand when it's time to upgrade to a twin bed? Will that toy-storage unit be able to live anywhere else in the house? Is this room for your first child, with the hope of more to come, or is it for your youngest? While it's ideal if you can choose items that'll have a second life in this room or another, it's perfectly fine to choose and use items that are just for now. However, promise yourself that you'll part with those pieces sans resistance when it's time (see "Six Ways to Get Rid of Things," page 55).

- **Put comfort first (or at the very least, not last).** When choosing chairs and beds, make sure they're sized and placed so that kids can get into and out of them easily. In other words, if you're looking for a sofa or chair to use at story time, it needs to accommodate two people without circus-worthy contortion acts, and don't choose a ladder bed if your kid can't comfortably climb in. Likewise, kids (and parents) love the idea of bunk beds, but test them out first to make sure the bottom-bunk dweller won't be bumping his or her head every morning.

- **Put on your paranoid-parent hat.** This is not an official guide to babyproofing, but please use common sense when selecting furniture for a kid's room. Don't underestimate any kid's strength and interest in climbing up, scrambling onto, or pulling down a heavy piece of furniture. Substantial, solid-construction furniture is OK and can actually be safer than lightweight "kid" furniture, but you'll need to secure everything that could possibly tip over to the wall using strap kits from the hardware store. Yes, you can screw bolts into that vintage highboy dresser if it'll keep it from toppling over. Safe design is good design!

➤➤ Simply framed but generously sized, a line drawing becomes a centerpiece above a nursery's marble mantel.

◀◀ A tot's room gets its color and personality from smaller pieces like a rug and pennant banner. The versatile upholstered bed can be styled to suit any number of decor and color themes as its now-wee occupant grows.

In the Details

Children have a way of focusing on the little things, so creating a comfortable, creativity-stoking kids' space they'll truly enjoy using often comes down to the minutiae. Think through the following components as you plan.

RUGS

Rugs aren't just soft on the feet, they can help dampen sound and keep a room from feeling drafty, both of which will increase the sense of comfort in the space. Shaggier, higher-pile floor coverings can be fun in children's bedrooms—kids love texture—but it's generally better to keep the pile low in true playrooms, as there will be less chance of the rug collecting errant Legos and graham-cracker crumbs. No matter how plush the floor covering, be sure to outfit the room with one rug large enough to cover nearly the entire space. When centered in the room, there should be just a foot or two of bare floor at the edges of the room. Ideally, the legs of the bed nearest the center of the room should sit fully on the rug, and there should be no easy-to-trip-on corners and edges in areas where kids frequently walk.

A wall-hung book rack stacked with kids' favorite titles doubles as playroom art. Two kid-friendly reading chairs complement the graphic prints and add vibrant color to the space.

There are no "boy" or "girl" colors.

TABLES AND SHELVES

There's no such thing as a completely kid- or babyproofed room, but you can avoid some of the bumps, falls, and boo-boos by opting for furniture with cushioned surfaces (think upholstered footstools and beds) and tables with rounded corners. Resist making trend-driven decisions like putting a ceramic garden stool in a nursery as an end table, as they're heavy and easy to break; also beware of tables with splayed-out legs, which can be easy to trip on. If the profile is right, though, the sky's the limit! Feel free to incorporate living room or adult bedroom furniture such as end tables with drawers for storage and bookshelves that can be stacked with both reading material and toys. Have fun with finishes, bringing in painted or metallic tables and storage pieces that add vibrancy and a layered (not matchy-matchy) look to the space. Testing out any ultra-bold choices in your room mock-up can help you find the right balance of color between walls, furniture, rugs, and art.

WINDOW TREATMENTS

Even more than in other rooms of the home, window treatments in kids' spaces should allow for full light control. Kids are extremely sensitive to daylight levels and sleep best in true darkness. Curtains or cordless Roman shades with a blackout lining are more available than ever before, so seek out these options if you can. (You can also turn any curtains you already have into blackout shades by adding a light-blocking liner or a blackout layer via a double curtain rod.) Choose or hem curtains so they hang slightly above the floor or graze it only slightly, just "kissing" the floor; longer curtains that "puddle" tend to look more formal and can pose a tripping risk, so while they can work for teens' or tweens' rooms, they're best avoided in toddlers' spaces.

While today's parents are more comfortable going beyond blue for boys, pink for girls, and green or yellow for we-don't-want-to-know, there's still a bias toward "gender-appropriate" tones. To which I say: Bleh. A rainbow-hued room can delight a five-year-old boy (see page 200), and rusty red can feel perfectly right for a toddler girl (page 188). If you're skittish about breaking color norms, pair an unconventional hue with a more expected theme (imagine a camel-and-charcoal palette featuring wooden trains for boys, or a fairy-themed girl's space dressed in fern green and earthy umber). Test your color choice in your room mock-up, starting with bedding or a wallpaper pattern that carries the theme. You might be surprised by how well it works.

➤➤ Wooden trains and figurines are not only fun to play with, but also fun to use as bedroom decor.

ART

Framed art and canvases can bring great life to a kid's space, but they're not the only options. Three-dimensional wall decor such as faux animal busts, paper pom-poms, and flag buntings can lend whimsy and tie together the room theme too. Whatever you choose, affix each piece to the wall securely so it can't be pulled down easily. Kids' own crafts are another possibility; incorporating chalkboards, a series of empty frames or clips, or floating shelves into your room plan can provide opportunities for kids to display their own masterpieces.

STORAGE

Baskets and bins are a playroom's best friend, especially when they coordinate with the decor. Use them to store rolled-up blankets, stuffed animals, blocks, trains, or anything you have lying around en masse. Look for oversize woven or knit baskets with handles, which make it easy to move items (particularly toy sets) from one area to another.

A series of cheeky animal prints provides a focal point above a headboard-free bed in a kid's room.

CONCLUSION

Throughout this book, I've shared many a design revelation. If you walk away with just one epiphany, however, let it be this: Everyone deserves a home he or she loves. Everyone is capable of creating his or her haven; everyone has a style (even if your current place has, well, none). Like dressing yourself or learning to cook, refining your decorating style is all about practice. Whether your budget is high or low, and whether you have 100 square feet to decorate or 10,000, style at home is not about what you have, but how much you care.

I'll admit, the process isn't perfect and you *will* make decorating mistakes. Even professional designers and stylists don't always get it right every time—maybe the rug is too blue for the wall color, maybe the dining chairs are an inch too short for the table. But give it a shot. Slip up with a purchase or acquisition? Return it, sell it, or give it to someone, then try something else. Let your home be a living, breathing expression of yourself, your life, and your style today.

HAPPY DECORATING!

ACKNOWLEDGMENTS

Endless thanks to Joyelle West, whose lens elevated every inch of this book. Thanks to Kathleen Jayes, my editor at Rizzoli, for shepherding this work onto bookshelves (and, I hope, coffee tables) everywhere. Thanks to designer Laura Palese, who understood my hopes and painstakingly brought them to life. Thanks to Joy Tutela of the David Black Agency, for being a relentless believer, coach, and advocate; may there be many more Acela rides in our future.

Thanks to all of the inspired and generous friends who opened their doors to Joyelle and me: Alisa Goldberg, Meredith Mahoney, Jane Rawnsley Peterson, Kelly Lorenz, Chloe and Zev Rosen, Cristy and Alex Beram, Courtney and Rob Favelukes, Jamie and Jon-Luc Dupuy, Emily Starr Alfano, Lindsey Graziano, Suzanne and Ryan Hale, Courtney Webster, and my sister Christine Crowley. You are living the message of this book.

I'm grateful to Olivia Rassow and Lizi Ham for their styling assistance, Keriann Coffey for all of the feedback and fodder, and Kaitlin Madden for the initial spark to write a book at all. *Bisous*.

Thank you everyone at Joss & Main and Wayfair who showed their support: Zac Bernstein, Adrienne Brown, Karen Sen, Jayme Huber, Grace Heintz, Rebekah Gallacher, Caroline Burns, Jane Carpenter, Kyle Wright. Thank you, Paul Toms, for your early, amused backing; thank you, John Mulliken, for dragging me into this messy, fabulous world of e-commerce and decor. Tell me, guys, what are we going to do next?

Thanks to Rizzy Home for granting me use of your chic pillow pattern on the spine and cover, and Little Seeds for permission to feature your nursery makeover on pages 54 and 193.

Finally, thanks to Mom for teaching me that your home is a place of pride and protection, and that everyone should know how to use a needle and thread. *Grazie*, Dad, for believing I had something to say and reading through all of it with a minimum of snark. Thanks to Anna and Christine (again) for the support I always feel, even when the months and miles get between us. Thanks to Sarah Pirker for keeping both my home and my children humming while I worked. And thanks, of course, to Dave, Sarah, and Jonah. You are my home.

First published in the United States of America in 2018

by Rizzoli International Publications, Inc.

300 Park Avenue South

New York, NY 10010

www.rizzoliusa.com

Photography © Joyelle West

Jacket and interior design by Laura Palese

2017 2018 2019 2020 / 10 9 8 7 6 5 4 3 2 1

Distributed in the U.S. trade by Random House, New York

Printed in China

ISBN-13: 978-0-8478-6179-8

Library of Congress Catalog Control Number:
2017957096